PENGUIN BOOKS

LOVING YOUR CHILD IS NOT ENOUGH

Nancy Samalin received her M.S. and professional diploma in counseling from Bank Street College of Education. She studied with Dr. Alice Ginott for ten years and founded her own Parent Guidance Workshops. Since 1976, she has trained more than 2,500 parents, and her work has been the subject of articles in *McCall's*, *New York* magazine, *The New York Times*, and *Parents* magazine. Samalin is on the adjunct faculty at Bank Street College of Education and the New School for Social Research. She has two children and lives with her husband in New York.

Author of *Cara: Growing with a Retarded Child*, Martha Moraghan Jablow has written for *Parents* magazine, *The New York Times*, *Working Woman*, and other publications. She lives in Philadelphia with her husband and two children.

LOVING YOUR CHILD IS NOT ENOUGH

Positive Discipline That Works

NANCY SAMALIN

with Martha Moraghan Jablow

PENGUIN BOOKS

PENGUIN BOOKS
Published by the Penguin Group
Viking Penguin Inc., 40 West 23rd Street,
New York, New York 10010, U.S.A.
Penguin Books Ltd, 27 Wrights Lane, London W8 5TZ, England
Penguin Books Australia Ltd, Ringwood,
Victoria, Australia
Penguin Books Canada Ltd, 2801 John Street,
Markham, Ontario, Canada L3R 1B4
Penguin Books (N.Z.) Ltd, 182–190 Wairau Road,
Auckland 10, New Zealand

Penguin Books Ltd, Registered Offices: Harmondsworth,
Middlesex, England

First published in the United States of America by Viking Penguin Inc. 1987
Published in Penguin Books 1988

LIBRARY OF CONGRESS CATALOGING IN PUBLICATION DATA
Samalin, Nancy.
Loving your child is not enough: positive discipline that works/
Nancy Samalin with Martha Moraghan Jablow.
p. cm.
Reprint. Originally published: New York, N.Y., U.S.A.: Viking,
1987.
Bibliography: p.
Includes index.
ISBN 0 14 00.9473 3
1. Discipline of children. 2. Child rearing. 3. Parenting.
I. Jablow, Martha Moraghan. II. Title.
[HQ770.4.S26 1988]
649'.64—dc 19 87-29199

Printed in the United States of America by
R. R. Donnelley & Sons Company, Harrisonburg, Virginia
Set in Janson

To Dr. Alice Ginott, without whom this book could never have been written. She has been my mentor, teacher and catalyst for change, to whom my family and I owe an enduring debt of gratitude.

AND

To Sy, whose love, faith and unwavering belief in me have been a source of joy and growth for all the time we have been together.

ACKNOWLEDGMENTS

Without the generosity, courage and openness of the parents in my groups, this book could never have been written. I thank each and every one of them for their willingness to share their successes and struggles with me. I only wish I could acknowledge each of them in person.

My sons, Eric and Todd, have been my willing and unwilling guinea pigs with such a good grace for the past two decades. I wish to thank them for all they have taught me about being a parent.

Sy has held my hand every step of the way, and provided endless love and comfort in the face of my highs and lows.

Working with Martha has been a special privilege. Not only is she a true professional, but her levelheadedness, her responsiveness and sensitivity and her ability to act as a sounding board helped to clarify and articulate this approach. She has taught me what it means to work as a team.

Nan Graham, my editor at Viking Penguin, has been the guiding spirit behind this book. Her enthusiasm, discriminating ear, thoroughness and deep understanding of and belief in the value of these ideas have made working with her an enriching experience.

My agents, Philippa Brophy and Sterling Lord, have been an invaluable help, for which I am extremely appreciative.

There are many people who have made it possible for me to offer my classes to the public and who have demonstrated their longstanding support of my work. In particular I wish to acknowledge Carla Stevens at The New School for Social Research, Susan Ginsberg at Bank Street College of Education, and Rabbi Harlan Wechsler at Park Avenue Synagogue.

I am deeply indebted to the following people who have so generously given of their time, contributed invaluable advice and encouraged the development of this project from its inception. Ellen Galinsky went out of her way to be helpful, as did Jane Hirschmann, Leonard Weinstock, Frank Porter, Marsha Riklis Hirschfeld, Madeleine Friedlander, Ellen Zanetti, Arlette Brauer, Elaine Koster, Dorothy Jordon, Suzanne Guglielmi, Ron Wolin and Jean Soichet. I'd also like to thank Bob McGrath for permission to use his anecdote and Brandon Himmel for his food chart.

I am most grateful to my parents and first teachers, Elizabeth and Irving Kaufmann and Phillip and Ruth Hettleman, who have given me my values and encouraged my determination and persistence.

Author's Note

In my workshops, parents bring in dialogues that they have had with their children and we talk about ways to improve their communication. In this book, to protect their privacy, I have changed all of the names of the parents and children and anything which might identify them in the dialogues. Where the words and the conversations have been altered, the spirit of the dialogues is true.

CONTENTS

Loving Your Child
Is Not Enough

Introduction

When my two children were asleep, I often looked fondly on their sweet, serene faces and thought how much I loved them. But when they were awake—spilling milk, pulling tuna fish cans off the supermarket shelves, hitting each other with blocks, failing spelling tests, whining and clinging to me when I wanted to show them off—I was anything but a loving parent. I nagged, screamed, criticized, labeled, threatened, punished and constantly felt guilty about the words I used, words I would never have imagined saying to another human being. I had lots of love and good intentions but, without skill, they were not enough to change my children's behavior. Our typical conversations frequently erupted into hostile confrontations:

Me: Eric, watch out. You'll spill the juice.
Eric: No, I won't.
Me: You've done it before and you'll do it again. Why do you always leave the glass on the edge of the table?
Eric: Stop nagging and leave me alone.

A minute later, over went the juice.

Me: Damn it, Eric! Why don't you watch out? You are so clumsy. I've told you a million times about this. Now clean up this mess!

I had been a teacher before I had children and I expected to be as patient with my own children as I had been with my students. But I discovered that being a parent was the most difficult, frustrating job in the world. I wanted to be an accepting, nurturing parent—the great earth mother—but I was totally unprepared for the reality of coping with two active, imperfect children. I found that I had a terrible temper and amazingly little self-control. I wanted to be empathic, but I was critical. I wanted the boys to get along well, but they were always quarreling. I didn't want to talk too much, but I never shut up. I wanted them to treat me with respect, but they talked back to me. I wanted them to listen, but they tuned me out.

I searched for answers and read volumes of childrearing advice. Everything sounded so easy and I resolved to reform my behavior: "Today I will discipline without screaming." But as soon as my sons began grabbing at the precarious piles of pears at the grocery, I turned into the instant harpy again. I fell back into my old, habitual "on automatic" ways because I had no idea of what to do instead. I could not translate all those platitudes, "be consistent . . . don't play favorites . . . be patient and accepting," into specific techniques. I desperately needed concrete alternatives.

When my sons were seven and eight, I joined a mothers' workshop led by the gifted psychologist, Dr. Alice Ginott, who was continuing the work of her late husband, Dr. Haim Ginott. In these workshops I became acutely aware of the effect my words were having on my children: "Watch out. You'll spill the juice" made Eric feel clumsy so he became defensive—"No, I won't"—and set up a self-fulfilling prophecy: over goes the juice. I attacked his self-image—"Why do you always leave the glass on the edge . . ."—and made him defiant—"Stop nagging and leave me alone." My words did not inspire him to move the glass.

Over time, as I learned to catch myself before uttering my automatic responses and I began to hear my children differently, the atmosphere started to change dramatically in our family. I did not learn new alternatives to yelling, threatening and criticizing overnight. Acquiring any worthwhile skill is a process that takes time and practice. And it won't work for you every time. But if it works even 10 percent of the time, that is better than nothing. Our sons are now twenty and twenty-one and as a result of the skills I learned from Dr. Ginott, we have built a relationship of mutual respect, trust and appreciation.

As I saw what an enormous difference skills and information could make within my own family, I wanted to share this powerful knowledge with other parents who, like me a few years earlier, had no alternatives to lecturing, punishing or bribing their children into obedience. I believed that other parents could benefit as I had from a knowledge of these skills, so after fourteen years of teaching, I earned an advanced degree in counseling and founded Parent Guidance Workshops in New York City. My goal was to help parents become more aware of the way they talk, see the effect of their words and begin to respond in new ways to improve relationships with their children. And it worked. By communicating in new ways, it *is* possible to promote cooperation instead of resentment, to express anger without hurting or insulting and to set limits on behavior while responding empathically to feelings.

In my weekly workshops, parents bring in written dialogues that they have had with their children and together we analyze these dialogues. By examining them, parents begin to listen to themselves. Listening is the key. When they begin to hear how ineffective or hurtful their impulsive, automatic responses can be, parents learn to substitute more caring and effective means of communicating. This book is based on the dialogues and experiences of thousands of parents who have participated in my workshops over the past decade. I am convinced that readers can learn from listening to my workshop parents.

As parents we are all plagued with the same dreary and demoralizing battles about eating, dressing, homework, television, sharing, chores, sibling fights, putting away toys and clothes. The dialogues I have chosen for this book were written by real parents facing these daily issues. The dialogues serve as models to illustrate how often our normal responses backfire and how other alternatives can improve our children's behavior, deepen rapport and help us enjoy the time we have with them.

1

Avoiding Daily Battles

If you could wear a concealed tape recorder for an entire day—or just half an hour—you might be amazed to hear the replay:

"Wake up . . . Get dressed . . . Change your shirt . . . Finish your cereal . . . Sit up straight . . . Brush your hair . . . Don't forget your lunch . . . Hurry up or you'll miss the bus . . . Practice your piano . . . Put your toys away . . . Get started on your homework . . . Wash up . . . Come to dinner right now . . . Put your napkin in your lap . . . Finish your rice . . . Take your bath . . . Put on your pajamas . . . Brush your teeth . . . Leave your sister alone . . . Get into bed . . . Turn out your light this minute!"

So much of our communication with children is simply "maintenance talk." Most parents are unaware of the incessant barrage of commands they give children. Is it any wonder that children become parent-deaf?

When we become parents, we assume that we are supposed to be twenty-four-hour-a-day teachers, forever working to improve our children. While teaching appropriate behavior and setting limits are necessary, most parents resort to one teaching method: lecturing. Telling children what to do—talking *at* them—is natural because that is how we were taught as children. When we are not conscious of the words we are using with children, we are programmed like machines to be "on automatic," replaying the tapes that have been stored in our memories since childhood. However, most of our lecturing doesn't encourage two-way communication. It invites children either to defy us or ignore us, setting the stage for power struggles and confrontations. A typical morning scene:

Mom: Come on, Chip. Get dressed for school now.
Chip: *(whining)* You dress me. I can't do it.
Mom: You certainly can. You're just being lazy.
Chip: No, I'm not.
Mom: You are five years old. You should be able to dress yourself.
Chip: I am not five yet. I'm four and three-quarters!
Mom: Oh, for God's sake! Benjy already dresses himself and he's only three and a half. Now get a move on or we'll be late.
Chip: I don't care.
Mom: *(yanking a shirt over Chip's head)* I'm sick of your nonsense.
Chip: *(in tears)* You're mean. I hate you.

Occasions for daily battles like this are plentiful—dressing, eating, doing homework, watching television, stalling at bedtime . . . These routine events easily escalate from minor skirmishes to major battles—which neither parent nor child wins. When we "win," we lose. When we make children obey by force, threats or punishment, we make them feel helpless. They can't stand feeling helpless, so they provoke another confrontation to prove they still have some power, as Chip did.

If Chip's mother had listened to her words, what would she have heard? "You're just being lazy" was a label that belittled Chip. He resented it and therefore denied it ("No, I'm not").

"You should be able to dress yourself" was a criticism that

also raised the stakes of their argument. Instead of complacently agreeing with her, Chip fought her with fact ("I'm four and three-quarters"). When her frustration led her to compare Chip with a younger child ("Benjy already dresses himself"), Chip's self-esteem was undercut and he replied with the defensive "I don't care." And when their power struggle peaked with Mother's "I'm sick of your nonsense," Chip could only react with tearful defiance—"You're mean. I hate you"—to express his revenge on Mom for "winning" the dressing battle.

Throughout this book, as I suggest new alternatives to the "on automatic" responses like those Chip's mother used, I stress the need to be permissive with children's feelings, yet strict about their behavior. This is not a book for indulgent parents—it is possible to be authoritative without being authoritarian. Our goals are to increase rapport with our children, to diminish our negative responses and theirs and to promote their cooperation and self-esteem. We will never be able to avoid conflicts entirely because parents' needs and children's needs are so often opposed. When we need to hurry, they want to dawdle. When we crave ten minutes of solitude after a trying day, they issue eighteen demands for immediate attention. When we get a long-distance phone call, they interrupt us with a crisis. When we are feeling pressured to fix dinner for guests, they're assembling an army of action figures on the dining-room table.

If we can enjoy our children even five more minutes a day and yell or criticize five minutes less, we are moving in the right direction. We may not be able to fix every situation perfectly, but we can diminish daily battles by substituting new words. The particular words we speak determine the way children react. In the following example, Jenny's mother responded on automatic at first. But after she took some time to rethink her words, she was able to respond more effectively:

Jenny: I don't want Sally to come to my birthday party.
Mom: But you know that Sally is your friend.
Jenny: No, she's not.
Mom: That's not a nice thing to say. How would Sally feel if she heard you?
Jenny: I don't care. She's not coming.
Mom: So maybe you shouldn't have a party at all.
Jenny: Okay, no party.

Mother first denied Jenny's feelings by saying, "You know that Sally is your friend." Jenny clearly didn't want Sally at the party but her mother contradicted her without exploring why Jenny felt that way. "That's not a nice thing to say. How would Sally feel . . ." is preaching. When parents lecture, children tune out, as Jenny's "I don't care" proved.

Many parents resort to threats when they don't know what else to do. ("So maybe you shouldn't have a party at all.") But you are then boxed in: you must either follow through with the threat, against your better judgment, or back down. If you back down, you convince your child not to take you seriously again. Neither choice is effective discipline. Jenny reacted to the threat of a canceled party by cleverly calling her mother's bluff: "Okay, no party." At this point, both were deadlocked in a power struggle that neither could win.

A while later, Jenny's mother tried another tack by using some of the techniques we will discuss in this book:

Mom: It seems to me that something about Sally disturbs you.
Jenny: Yeah, she always plays with my dolls.
Mom: And that really bothers you.
Jenny: Yes. I don't like her to.
Mom: Well, can you think of a way that will solve this problem at the birthday party?
Jenny: Well, maybe if I put my dolls away in my room

and we had the party downstairs, she won't want to play with them. Then she could come to the party.

Mom: Great idea!

Does this sound too good to be true? Let's examine what Jenny's mother did. By saying, "It seems to me that something about Sally disturbs you," she recognized and gave value to Jenny's feelings. Her words also allowed Jenny an opening to reveal what was bothering her. When her mother acknowledged Jenny's right to feel the way she did, by saying "And that really bothers you," Jenny felt that her mother truly understood her. Jenny's mother used the skill of acknowledging feelings to draw out information that helped identify the problem. And she gave Jenny the opportunity to be a problem solver by asking, ". . . can you think of a way . . . ?" If Jenny hadn't come up with a solution, Mother might have suggested two or three possibilities and allowed Jenny to choose one. When given the opportunity to become problem solvers, children gain self-knowledge. Not only does this enhance their self-confidence, but they are also more likely to follow through on a solution that they have suggested themselves than one we have spoon-fed them.

As you read these dialogues I have collected from parents who have been waging the same daily battles you have, please keep in mind that there is no single, perfect response for each situation. You know your child better than anyone else does. Each child is unique and may respond differently to the same situation or statement. What works beautifully with your younger child may backfire with your older one. And what worked well today with one child may not work with him tomorrow.

As you begin to use some of these new techniques to respond to your child, you can be imaginative and creative (if you have the energy at that moment!). Most parents are so predictable that children know what we will say before we even open our mouths. So before we start talking, it is helpful to stop and question: "Are my words going to cause confrontation or cooperation?" . . . "Do I want to set a firm limit here or is this not worth struggling about?" . . . "Would I say what I am about to say if this were someone else's child?"

Which Battles Are Worth Fighting?

What is really important? How children look? What they wear? What they eat? How they feel about themselves? What grades they earn? How well they perform at sports? What others think of them and how that reflects on us? If we were to make a list of what bugs us most about children's behavior, it might be endless: "He daydreams, whines, forgets to tuck in his shirt, kicks the table leg during every meal, acts fresh, never washes until reminded eleven times, is pokey about doing chores, plays with food, fights with his sister and brother, interrupts me constantly, always ignores me when I call . . ."

Some parents have found it helpful to write down a "bug list" of the annoying behaviors that most often lead to conflict. Examining the list helps them gain some perspective and enables them to zero in on the serious offenses while relaxing about the lesser issues. One father curbed his excessive demands on his children by asking himself, "Will this really matter a week from today?" Other parents ask, "Can I avoid this? Is it worth fighting about? How important is it if Johnny goes to bed in pajamas or underpants?" Others have found it useful to jot down all the demands they make on their children in the course of a day; after examining the list, they find it easy to eliminate the less necessary demands. Naturally every parent has different priorities and can choose those that are most important.

Another strategy to avoid or diminish daily skirmishes is

to be flexible when you can. Alison, five, and Amanda, three, were arguing about where to sit at the table; Mother decided to be flexible instead of locking horns with them:

Alison: Amanda is sitting in my place.
Amanda: I want to sit here tonight.
Alison: It is my seat. You can't sit there.
Amanda: Yes, I can. And I am.
Alison: MommEEEEE! Amanda is in my chair. It is not fair. It's my place.

This was not a new scene in Alison and Amanda's home. Mother usually picked up Amanda and moved her to another chair. Amanda always screamed and a struggle ensued. But this time, Mother tried a different response:

Mom: *(to Alison)* You really like to sit there all the time.
Alison: Yes.
Mom: But Amanda likes to sit there, too, and maybe it's her turn tonight.
Alison: I'll only give her my seat if I can sit over there.

"Over there" was the side of the table that was pushed against the wall.

Mom: Well, okay. Let's move the table out from the wall.

Mother did something special and unexpected for Alison by moving the table. Her short comment, "You really like to sit there all the time," avoided a scene and showed Alison that her mother accepted her feelings.

About five o'clock, when her daughters were tired and hungry, Jane and Cindy's mother was trying to write some long overdue letters. But the girls kept interrupting her with petty requests.

Jane: Where's the Monopoly game?

Mom: You can find it yourselves.

Cindy: But I want you to help us find it.

Mom: Can't you girls just leave me in peace for ten min-
          utes so I can finish these letters? I can't concentrate
          when you bother me with all your questions.

Jane: When are you going to start cooking dinner? I'm
          starving.

Mom: I'll be able to start it sooner if you'll stop inter-
          rupting me.

Mother was about to blow up when she realized that she
could use flexibility to assuage this escalating scene. "Why
don't I finish the letters tonight when they are in bed?" she
asked herself. When she relayed this incident to one of our
workshop groups, Jane and Cindy's mother said, "It wasn't
that I was giving them their way. But I realized that I had
choices—the letters could wait. And I could enjoy writing
them more when the girls were in bed."

When It Isn't Negotiable

Parents can afford to be flexible when they've decided that
an issue isn't important enough to fight about. But there are
many times when parents do need to set clear limits, to be
firm rather than flexible. In the process of setting limits, you
can be authoritative and still avoid a confrontation, as Mike's
mother did:

Mike: Mommy, make me scrambled eggs with cheese.

Mom: Okay, honey.

After the eggs were cooked:

Mike: I'm not eating these eggs. They aren't what I wanted.

Mom: Oh, that's what I thought you wanted.

Mike: Well, it's not. Make me something else.

Mom: I only make breakfast once. You can eat it if you want to.

Mike: *(looking surprised)* Oh, well . . . okay.

And he began to eat the eggs.

The result may sound too good to be true, and it might not always work so easily, but Mike's mother avoided a battle without caving in to his demands. Had she been on automatic, she would have ordered, "Eat the eggs! You asked for them and that's what you'll eat." When he said, "They aren't what I wanted," she did not deny his statement but stated *her* perception: ". . . that's what I thought you wanted." This statement did not attack him as "You said you wanted them" would have done. If she had begun with "You . . ." Mike would have been put in a defensive position and would have undoubtedly come back with an argument.

When he demanded that she cook something else, she firmly set the limit: "I only make breakfast once." But she did not box him in either. She gave him a choice ("You can eat them if you want to") rather than an order which he would have been tempted to defy. Mike decided to eat the eggs he'd requested when he realized that refusing them wouldn't get the usual rise out of his mother. Her response is not a way to guarantee a child's eating his food—it is an example of how one mother skillfully avoided becoming enmeshed in a win-lose power struggle.

Consequences

Consequences are often more effective teachers than all our lectures and threats. If Jack habitually forgets to put his favorite jeans into the laundry, they won't be clean for school next week. If Roger doesn't come to the table when called, his spaghetti will be cold and congealed. If Alice doesn't button her jacket and put on her mittens, the brisk wind will remind her more convincingly than all her mother's nagging. If Darren doesn't finish his homework, he'll be unprepared when the teacher calls on him tomorrow. If parents say nothing in these instances, children will learn from the consequences rather than spending their energy bickering with us.

John's mother constantly fought with her eleven-year-old son about getting up in the morning. Finally she realized that allowing him to be late to class would be much more persuasive than all her wake-up calls. She explained to him that she would no longer be responsible for getting him up. From then on, he set his alarm clock instead of depending on his mother to get him to school on time. He was late much less frequently.

"What Can I Do to Get My Kid to Listen?"

That question is usually the first one asked by parents in my workshops. The answer is brief: talk less. Children are so accustomed to lengthy orders from parents that they quickly become parent-deaf. As one young boy said, "When my mom gets to the second sentence, I forget what she said in the first." Another child said, "Mommy, whenever I ask you a little question, you always give me such a big answer." If you can stop yourself at the end of the first sentence, you can elicit more cooperative responses and avoid many a daily battle.

If you can think in terms of what I call the "one-word rule," you can get into the habit of being brief. For example, Phil came in from the rain and tracked muddy puddles across the kitchen floor. If she were on automatic, his mother would have said, "How many times have I told you to take your boots off on the porch? Look at this mess you've made! You think I have all the time in the world to spend mopping up floors? You're inconsiderate and careless. Why can't you re-member something as simple as taking off your boots out-side? . . ." Phil would have tuned out after the first sentence. Instead, his mother can deliver the message simply and ef-fectively without criticism that will cause Phil's resentment. She needs to say only one word: "BOOTS!"

Rather than endlessly "reminding," a euphemism for "nag-ging" ("You forgot to brush your teeth again. Why are you so forgetful? You'll have a mouthful of cavities. Your brother never forgets to brush his teeth . . ."), you can simply say, "TEETH!"

A single word may need to be repeated, perhaps in a stronger tone, but even when it is, there are no criticisms or hidden messages. The one-word rule is effective because it

For Better or For Worse
by Lynn Johnston

For Better or For Worse
Copyright 1983 Universal Press Syndicate.

addresses the situation, not the child. The situation can't argue back. But a child who feels blamed will either turn off or defend herself and mobilize her resistance toward her parents.

Children resist orders just as they resist verbiage. As my son once admitted, "Mom, whenever you give me an order, I want to do just the opposite." They respond much more positively to a brief, impersonal *description of what needs to be done* than to a long-winded accusation, threat or command:

	Rather than
"The library book is five days overdue."	"Take that book back to the library right after school today. Don't you know it's five days overdue already?"
"The school bus will be here in ten minutes."	"Get your coat. Don't forget your bookbag. Hurry up! NOW! You are so slow."
"Coats belong in the closet, not on the floor."	"Pick up that coat this minute! Why are you so sloppy? Didn't you ever hear of a coat hanger?"
"The hamster's cage needs cleaning."	"You never remember to clean your hamster's cage! Don't you care about your pets? Clean it out immediately or you can't go out and play with Sandy."
"You had fun with Danny	"If you don't come to the

but now it's time to go home."

door right this minute, I won't let you come to Danny's house ever again. Do you hear me?"

"Grandma must be spoken to with respect."

"You're so rude. Don't you dare talk back to me or be fresh to your grandmother again, ever!"

Parents can help children learn without making them feel inadequate in the process. Sometimes if we walk away after briefly stating our expectations, we make it easier for a child to cooperate. A child has difficulty saving face if we stand over him like a drill sergeant, waiting for instant obedience. After he spills his milk, we can simply say, "Here's the sponge. The spill needs to be cleaned up"—and then walk away to let him maintain his dignity.

Fight Starters

Mom: Toby! Get in here! Toby! NOW! You are getting messier every day. Your room is a pigsty. If you're going to throw your clothes around like this, I'm not going to buy you any clothes at all. Why can't you be neater? Why can't you ever put your clothes away?

Toby: Why don't you ever yell at Jamie? His room is messy, too. You're not so neat yourself.

Certain words used AT THE BEGINNING OF A SENTENCE—"You," "If," and "Why"—are like red flags waved in front of a child. They invite a child to charge into battle. Instead of agreeing with her mother that her room was untidy and willingly cleaning it up, Toby fought back. She tried to deflect the charges to her brother and she shot back her resentment at her mother with a counteraccusation: "You're not so neat yourself."

Toby's mother used all the red-flag words. *"You* are getting messier . . ." opened the attack. Sentences starting with "you" beg an adversarial reaction immediately. They attack the person, not the problem ("You always . . . You never . . . You'd better . . . You're such a . . .").

"If" is usually the beginning of a threat: *"If* you're going to throw your clothes around like this, I'm not going to buy you any clothes at all." Such threats are ineffective disciplinary tools. Does Toby's mother really intend never to buy another article of clothing for her daughter? Toby knows the answer, so it is an empty threat. Threats also set up power plays—a strong figure threatening a weaker one. And the weaker one hears it as a challenge and wants to strike back.

"Why" is usually the beginning of an accusation: *"Why* can't you be neater? Why can't you ever . . ." This kind of broad critical attack triggers a defensive or defiant reaction because it calls up all the child's previous misdeeds—as if Toby had never in her life put a sweater in a drawer. (See Chapter 6 for a more extensive discussion of criticism.)

Instead of using "you," "if" and "why" to raise the issue of Toby's messy room, her mother could have tried a brief description of what needed to be done: "Toby, the clothes need to be hung up. Clothes left in heaps will get wrinkled and need ironing."

AS SOON AS is a particularly effective phrase to substitute for "if" used as a threat. When you want your child to do something he doesn't want to do, "as soon as" is a nonthreatening motivator: *"As soon as* the clothes are picked up, we can go to the store together." *When* used in a similar context can have the same effect: *"When* all the homework is done, then you can watch your hour of TV." Even young children who have inaccurate concepts of time can understand the sequence of "as soon as" or "when . . . , then . . ." Rather than setting up a situation in which a powerful person threatens a less powerful one, we can strike a partnership ("As soon as you do A, then I'll do B.") and we can turn a potential power struggle into a cooperative effort. "As soon as" may not sound very different from "if," but parents have told me how often it does work—much to their surprise. They say that "as soon as" changes their tone of voice and is less provocative than "if."

Choices

Giving children a choice about what they can wear, what they will eat, when they will do a job, helps them feel competent about making decisions and solving problems. And giving them choices is another way to diminish daily struggles. Rather than ordering, lecturing or threatening, you might say, "Would you rather take your bath before or after supper?" or "I need your help. Either you can set the table or you can empty the dishwasher. You decide." When a child is given a choice, she doesn't feel that she is a lowly subject bossed about by a mighty ruler. But in giving choices, parents need to take care not to threaten in the guise of "choice." If the only real choice is between a punishment and something that the parent wants the child to do, it is actually no choice at all. It is simply a threat: "Either you take your little brother to the park right now, or you stay home from the movies tonight."

Offering a child a valid choice will not only help prevent a problem from becoming a major showdown, but it will also help him become a competent decision maker. Mark, twelve, and his father had frequent blowups about the use of tools in Dad's workshop:

Dad: Mark, would you please put the drill bits back in their box or we won't be able to find them the next time we need the drill?

Mark: I'm not your slave. You were using them, too.

Dad: That's not the point. We were doing this project together. If you want to do another part of this cleanup job, then we'll talk about it.

Mark: Like what?

Dad: Well, you could sweep up the sawdust or put away the drill bits.

Mark: I guess I'd rather sweep up the sawdust 'cause then I get to use the hand vacuum.

Mark's father did not get sidetracked by his son's provocative phrase, "I'm not your slave." He reiterated the basic rules of the workshop—cleaning up and putting tools away. By offering Mark a choice and staying calm, he was an effective disciplinarian. Staying calm when provoked and offering choices to gain cooperation rather than yelling a threat are difficult to do—as every parent knows.

One of the easiest places to illustrate how choices can defuse daily battles is the dinner table. Few parents give children real choices about selecting food. When we become parents, most of us become instant nutritionists insisting on what, when and how much children should put in their stomachs regardless of their hunger level or individual taste. But this pattern leads to many an unnecessary battle.

A mother who served traditional dinners for years finally grew tired of her children's constant moaning:

Frank: Nothing you cook is any good.

Sandy: You know we hate mashed potatoes.

Gloria: Why do we have to eat this yucky meat?

Exhausted by the unpleasantness around mealtime, Mother decided to surprise her children one evening by serving dinner in bowls and on platters, rather than dishing out separate portions to each child.

Mom: From now on, you may have as much or as little as you want. The only rule is "Don't put anything on your plate that you don't want to eat."

Dubious at first, they tested her for the next few days. Sandy chose no potatoes or vegetables. Frank placed one pea on his plate and looked at her to see how she would react. Mother continued to say nothing and the children gradually began to eat from hunger. For the first week or so they didn't eat a perfectly balanced diet, but mealtimes became more enjoyable and less of a battleground, and the children did eat vegetables eventually.

Perhaps some parents may not wish to go as far as this mother did to rearrange their style of serving meals. But even simple food choices help prevent battles: "Would you like your carrots cooked or raw?" or "Would you like a cheese or peanut butter sandwich?" We can decide what to buy and serve but we can avoid mealtime struggles by giving children reasonable choices within our parameters. When children are given mealtime choices, power struggles are not only diminished, but children are also getting an important message from their parents: "We value and respect your taste, judgment and individual differences."

A mother who described her effort "to eliminate some of our crazy food problems" suggested to her nine-year-old son that he make a menu for the week. She reported, "He went into his room, was silent and busy for almost an hour and came out and handed me a chart of his preferences." (See food chart, page 22.)

Letting the Child Solve the Problem

When we consult children and ask for their suggestions they will often come up with surprisingly effective solutions that

Sun.	Mon	Tues.	Wed.
☐ French toast ⊞	☐ egg OJ	☐ French toast ⊞	☐ French toast OJ
O strawberrys OJ	◊ chicken soup	◊ Ellio's Pizza OJ	◊ Chicken ✿⊞
◊ Chicken soup ⊞	D Popcorn	D cherrys	⊞ D strawberrys
D Apple			

Thurs.	Fri.	S at.	**Key**
☐ egg ⊞	☐ egg ⊞	☐ Pancakes ⊞	☐ = Breakfast O = Lunch ◊ = Dinner OJ = Orange Juice ⊞ = Grape Juice D = Disert ✿ = Crispee cKicken ⊠ = Suprise ◚ = Suprise Drink ⊞ = Bagel if I want
◊ Shrimp OJ	◊ Hot dog ⊞	O Bagel OJ	
D Froz- Fruit	D apple	◊ ⊠ ◚	

avert major confrontations. If given opportunities to become problem solvers, children grow in self-confidence and they are more likely to follow through on a solution they have suggested than one we have dictated.

Mom: Honey, I really have to go now. I'm late. I asked you half an hour ago to get ready for bed and you're still playing. It's embarrassing for me always to be the last mommy to walk in after my class has started. What can we do?

Marissa: What time is it now?

Mom: It's eight o'clock and my class starts at eight.

Marissa: Hurry up, Mom. Don't worry about me. I'll get myself to bed.

She got up, pulled her night clothes from the closet and began to undress.

Mom: Thanks, honey. I appreciate your cooperation.

Mom: I am really fed up with these dirty clothes strewn all around your room. Every time I ask you to pick them up, we get into a fight. What can we do about this? Any ideas?

Don: Well, you could let me have the hamper in my room instead of the bathroom.

Mom: Why not? Let's move it into your room right now.

All Don's dirty clothes didn't end up in the hamper, but his mother appreciated even the 50 percent that did.

Three-and-a-half-year-old Will had been coming out of his room every night for weeks and complaining about the dark. His mother had tried every rational explanation about why there was nothing to fear, all to no avail. Then she decided to turn the solution back to him:

Will: It's too dark in my room.

Mom: You have a night-light.

Will: But I can't sleep.

Mom: What do you think we could do to help you stay in your room?

Will: What if you gave me my own flashlight, one of those big ones with a handle like Daddy's?

Mom: What a clever idea.

She lent him Daddy's flashlight that night and bought Will his own the next day. Will began staying in his room.

One caveat: Requesting a child's suggestions and moving toward mutually agreeable solutions work best when you are not in the midst of a problem. You are ahead of the game if you can anticipate a problem and ask children for solutions before the crisis erupts, as this father did after being repeatedly harassed about who sat where on every family car trip:

Dad: I want to talk with you kids about a problem we always have. Let's think about what to do before we even walk out the door. How can we avoid the fights about who sits up front?

Steve: I should sit up front because I'm the oldest.

Emily: That's not fair.

Mark: No, it's not. We should take turns.

Steve: Okay, but how will we keep track every time?

Emily: I have a new notebook. I'll write down each time we get in the car who sits where.

Mark: Yeah, that's fair. And we can keep the notebook in the car.

Steve: Okay, but I get the first turn today because I am the oldest.

Dad: Are you guys all agreed?

The children nodded and Dad reviewed the rules. It worked—at least for several weeks. Nothing works forever!

Some families formalize this problem-solving process by having a suggestion or complaint box or a family meeting to gather everyone's input. Once rules or solutions are agreed upon, it is wise to put them in writing and preferably post them in a prominent spot such as the refrigerator or bulletin board. One family with several boys discussed the need for a dry bathroom floor and toilet seat, made a sign and posted it above the toilet: "We aim to please. You aim, too, please."

In a family where television was a constant source of friction, Mother and Father decided to limit the amount of TV watching in consultation with their children. The mutually-agreed-upon solution was to reduce viewing to one hour on school nights with the children choosing the programs within that hour. They wrote down their choices and posted them next to the TV set.

Defusers

Three more techniques can defuse confrontations with children and help prevent numerous daily battles: giving advance information about a potentially difficult situation, using some fantasy or changing the mood with humor.

Giving children advance warning or information about what to expect can often avert problems. For instance, in anticipation of Grandmother's visit, Mother said to Laura, "Grandma is very self-conscious about her new hearing aid. How can we make sure not to hurt her feelings?" Laura replied, "Don't worry, Mom. I'll pretend I don't notice it." Mother not only gave Laura some valuable information in anticipation of a situation that could have become awkward, but she also made Laura feel grown-up and helpful.

Providing information about any potentially difficult situation can make a child more comfortable and can prevent a parent's having to "correct" a child in front of Grandma or anyone else. Children can cope much better with moving to a new town, visits to the doctor, dentist or hospital if we anticipate their questions and fears and give them clear information about what to expect. Artie's mother did this well:

Mom: I have some unpleasant news for you. We have to go to the doctor for a shot.
Artie: Oh, no.
Mom: I know it's not good news but we have to go.
Artie: Will it sting?
Mom: Yes, it might. But not for long.

At a workshop Artie's mother said that previous visits to the doctor had been nearly unbearable but this time "what could have been a threatening situation turned into a pleasant afternoon" because she prepared him for the visit rather than springing it on him. We wish every child would react as Artie did. But that's not always possible and we may just have to drag him, kicking and screaming, to the doctor. Hard as that is, at least we can help by sympathizing with his fear.

Other parents have related incidents of how advance preparation has averted problems when a child is about to go to sleep-away camp for the first time or even when a child is going to play at a friend's house where customs or disciplinary standards may be different from those at home.

Some parents also use timers as a way of giving children advance warning and avoiding a battle. For example, Patty always fussed whenever it was time to stop playing with a friend. Her mother tried—successfully—giving Patty notice: "I'm setting the timer for twenty minutes. When it rings, the playing will stop and we'll walk Michele home."

Other parents set the timer and play "beat the clock" to

help young children finish tasks, turning the chore into a race against time rather than a contest of wills.

Time is at the source of many daily battles. We often don't realize that time is very abstract to a young child. As Johnny said when his mother nagged him to hurry for the third time, "Mommy, I don't know how long ten minutes is." Timers, digital clocks and hourglasses offer visual ways of giving children concepts of time. When Johnny's mom put a digital clock in his room, he said, "Now I can see what ten minutes looks like."

Children love fantasy and it is another practical technique for avoiding arguments. After coming out of a movie,

Jill: Can we take a taxi home? The buses are so crowded.

Dad: *(about to say, "Boy, you sure are extravagant with my money," stopped himself and used a touch of fantasy instead)* Oh, if only I earned a million dollars a year, I'd flag a cab right now. In fact, if I had a million dollars, I'd buy you your own cab and hire a driver to take you wherever you want to go.

Jill: *(laughing)* Oh, Daddy, you're so ridiculous.

And they stepped onto a bus.

Fantasy allows parents to respond to children's endless desires in a gracious, playful way without putting them down or getting embroiled in prolonged arguments. You are still saying "no" but you are making the "no" more digestible. You can use a similar technique by suggesting that a child draw up a "wish list." Jonah's mother grew weary of his pleading for a new GI Joe figure every time they entered a shopping mall. Inevitably they got into a shouting match that ended with her declaring, "You have so many of those already. You're never satisfied!" She learned to avoid the usual fight when she said, "Well, that sounds like one to add to your wish list." This may not always work, but it often defuses our negative reactions to our children's endless demands.

A little drama can also diminish daily battles. When her child was giving her a stream of fresh backtalk, Mother raised her eyebrows theatrically and whispered, "I wonder why you're talking to me that way? I guess you've mixed me up with the Wicked Witch of the West." Her unexpected response changed the mood. Similarly, an unfamiliar or multisyllabic word can grab a child's attention and arouse his curiosity. When Roger and Ted were fighting, Dad distracted them by saying, "What a pugnacious pair you are." "What does *that* mean?" they asked, and forgot what they were fighting about.

The phrase "Let's erase that" can also be a defuser.

Martha saw herself headed for the habitual morning power struggle as her daughter dawdled through breakfast and dressing for school. Martha was well into her "hurry up" lecture and her tone of voice was rising.

Francine: *(putting her hands over her ears)* Stop bossing me!
Martha: Francine, let's erase what just happened.

Martha motioned with a sweep of her arm as if she were erasing a chalkboard. She left the room for a moment and reentered.

Martha: The school bus is due in fifteen minutes.

Francine finished her breakfast, put on her jacket and was ready for the bus on time. "Let's erase" demonstrates how just a few words can change the mood. "Let's erase" is a technique that needs to be used sparingly. But it can often prevent a battle from escalating.

Many parents tell me that morning dawdling and whining are their two greatest frustrations. The more we rush children, the more they dawdle. The more we carp about their whining, the louder they complain.

A fixed routine can help avert the morning hassles. We can lay out clothes the night before, set timers and use alarm clocks—but we need to accept the fact that on some days nothing will work and we'll all leave home frazzled. It would be marvelous if a few simple techniques could forever eradicate these headaches. But sometimes we have no options; we have to rush children because of the pressures on our own time.

Whining is like chalk scratching on a blackboard for most parents. Using the word "whine" ("Stop that whining!") reinforces it. It is more helpful to say, "Can you talk to me in your Annie voice?" or "in your big girl voice?"

Humor, another effective defuser of daily battles, is a way of not responding in kind to a child's provocation. Andy, four, became angry with his mother because she wouldn't take him to a store for a toy he desperately wanted.

Andy: I want it! If you don't get it for me, I'm going to cut off your head with an ax.

Mom: Aaargh! I'd look pretty funny walking around here without my head.

She pulled her turtleneck collar up over her face. Andy began to giggle and went outside to play without further argument.

Another mother tried to limit the amount of sweets her daughter ate and the arguments that sprang from this issue. She put the following note in the cookie jar:

> *Dear Phyllis,*
> *You've been caught! Only one per customer.*
> *Love,*
> *The Management*

Phyllis laughed when she found the note.

Putting a message in writing—particularly with a bit of humor—gets a point across to an older child with far less friction than a barrage of spoken orders. Karl's father was distressed by his son's habit of leaving baseball cards all over the living room. He tacked a note to Karl's door:

> *Dear Karl,*
> *I'm really tired of seeing your baseball cards all over the living-room floor. Please oblige.*
>
> > *Your pen pal,*
> > *Dad*

Karl then left a note on Dad's door:

> *Dear Dad,*
> *I'm really tired of finding the newspapers all over the living room all week long.*
>
> > *Your pencil pal,*
> > *Karl*

> *Dear Karl,*
> *The papers will be removed by Wednesday. Thanks for bringing it to my attention.*
>
> > *Love, Dad*

> *Dear Dad,*
> *The baseball cards will be kept in my room instead of in the living room.*
>
> > *Love,*
> > *Karl*

2

Acknowledging Feelings

How to Respond When Your Child Is Upset

Children can't help feeling what they do. When a child is angry, sad, jealous or afraid, many well-intentioned parents try to minimize or deny those feelings. But that backfires because the child feels misunderstood. When a child is upset or complaining, he needs a parent who can acknowledge his feelings. Acknowledging feelings is a skill that takes time and practice and doesn't come naturally to many of us because we want our child to be happy, not sad or angry or afraid.

Nine-year-old Sarah usually brought home excellent report cards that she enthusiastically showed her parents. But on the day she received her report card for the third quarter, she handed it to her father reluctantly:

Dad: What's the matter?
Sarah: It's not good.
Dad: Let me see. Sarah, it's a beautiful report card! What's wrong with it?
Sarah: It's not good. I hardly got any excellents.
Dad: Yes, you did. You got two. And everything else is good.

Sarah: *(sarcastically)* Sooooo?

Dad: It shows you are doing well in everything. I don't know why you're getting so upset. You have nothing to complain about. And your teachers' comments are terrific.

Sarah: But I only got a good in science and I did that extra credit project.

Dad: Well, why take it so personally? Maybe your teacher put the good on the report card before you turned in the project, or maybe she doesn't give excellents as easily as your other teachers.

Sarah: Soooo?

Dad: *(becoming angry and frustrated)* What more do you expect? This is a fine report card.

Sarah: No, it isn't.

She twisted her face into a pout and left the room, slamming the door behind her.

When children come to us with physical hurts, we know just what to do. We clean the wound and apply a bandage. But it is more difficult when they come to us with emotional hurts. Just as we want a physical injury to heal quickly, we also want their emotional distress "fixed" fast. In trying to comfort children when they are upset, we may unwittingly deny or minimize their feelings with such comments as "There's nothing to be afraid of," or "You don't have to act like it's the end of the world," or "It can't be *that* bad." Or, like Sarah's father, we try to eliminate their unhappiness and cheer them up by pointing out the sunny side (". . . it's a beautiful report card . . . everything else is good . . . your teachers' comments are terrific"). Sarah's father tried to talk her out of her feelings with logic and reasoning ("Maybe your teacher put the good on the report card before you turned in the project, or maybe she doesn't give excellents . . .").

When his attempts failed and led to an unwanted confrontation, he tried outright denial: "What more do you expect? This is a fine report card."

It is perfectly natural to want to pull children out of their distress, but in doing so we often make them more unhappy because our response convinces them that they aren't being heard. When we deny their feelings, they think we don't care about how they feel, and their frustration, anger or disappointment is then transferred to us. Sarah's sarcastic "Soooo?" and her parting pout were not so much directed at the disappointing report card as at her father who, she believed, didn't understand her.

Acknowledgment takes more than love and good intentions. It takes awareness and skill. When children are in the throes of strong emotions, our empathy lets them see us as their allies. After one parent in my workshop acquired the skill of acknowledging her son's feelings, she was astounded to hear him say, "Gee, Mom, you always used to be on my back and now you're on my side."

As natural as it is to want to protect children from unhappiness, we need to rethink our goals and our reasons for doing what we do. Rather than trying to make their distress "go away" by denying or contradicting their feelings, we need to be a sounding board for our children. But how can we do this? We can start by asking ourselves, "How would I feel if this were happening to me?" We can acknowledge their feelings by rephrasing their statements to let them know that we understand without sitting in judgment of them. The power of acknowledgment is that it gives us a concrete way to express empathy in words, as Paul's mother did when he came home from the first game of the basketball season. As soon as she saw his face, she knew his team had been defeated:

Paul: We lost. It was a disaster.

Mom: *(who was about to say, "Oh, it's not the end of the world. You've got the whole season ahead of you . . ." stopped herself and said instead)* You really look disappointed.

Paul: *(looking at her with surprise)* Yeah.

Mom: I know how much you were counting on winning today.

Paul: Yeah, I was. Oh, well, I guess it's not so bad. There'll be other games.

There is an interesting paradox in the outcome of this dialogue. Had his mother said, "It's not so bad. There'll be other games," Paul probably would have become angry with her for not taking his disappointment seriously and not empathizing with him. But her skillful responses ("You really look disappointed" and "I know how much you were counting on winning today") provided an effective sounding board for him. Once he felt understood, he was able to come to his own conclusion that this was not the tragic end of his basketball career. He, not his mother, was able to say, "I guess it's not so bad. There'll be other games." His words could be translated as "I guess I can cope with this disappointment after all."

Learning to respond empathically is a first and necessary step in helping children feel more competent. And isn't that what every parent wants—children who, when frustrated, enraged or disappointed, can cope with the situation instead of feeling helpless, depressed or anxious? But what makes acknowledgment difficult is that when they get upset, we get more upset and our emotions get in the way of our ability to recognize and accept their feelings.

Mario, ten, had been fidgeting at the kitchen table for fifteen minutes, chewing his pencil and grumbling about his math assignment. He suddenly flung the math book to the floor:

Mario: I can't do all this stupid homework. Add this, sub-
           tract that, multiply this, divide that.

Mom: It must be difficult to do a lot of work all day in
           school and then have to start all over again when
           you get home. You *do* have a lot of homework.

Mario looked at her with astonishment because he had expected her usual lecture ("Now just settle down and get
cracking. Complaining will only make it worse . . ."). All
Mario said was, "Right!" He picked up his book and began
plugging away at the math problems again. By reflecting
Mario's feelings of frustration, his mother provided an escape
valve for him so that Mario was able to move on and complete
his homework himself. His mother helped him with his assignment without looking at a single math problem. You can't
expect acknowledgment to change frustration into eagerness
every time; but when you do succeed, pat yourself on the back.

Polly came home from second grade and complained to
her father, "I forgot my notebook and the teacher yelled
at me."

Dad: That must have upset you.

Polly: Yes, it did. Frankie forgot his notebook and she
           didn't yell at *him*.

Dad: You felt it was unfair of her to yell at you and not
           at Frankie.

Polly: Right. She's mean.

Dad: You're pretty annoyed with her right now, aren't
           you?

Polly: I'd like to punch her in the nose and throw her in
           the garbage.

Dad: Boy, you *really* are angry with her.

At this point, Polly's mood seemed to lighten and she went
outside to roller-skate. Dad gave her what she needed: un-

derstanding rather than a lecture, and a chance to vent her anger with the teacher. His may not have been a "normal" reaction—when things go wrong, we sometimes automatically attack the child and tell her what's wrong with her. Polly's father did not. He didn't try to blame her for forgetting her notebook ("Well, it served you right. You deserved it"). Nor did he attempt to change her mind by preaching at a time when she was unable to listen to a sermon ("You shouldn't say she's mean . . . None of this would have happened if you'd just remembered your notebook"). By saying "You felt it was unfair of her to yell at you . . . ," he simply acknowledged her feelings without judging them. He knew it would be counterproductive to scold her again since the teacher had already done so.

If Dad had responded to Polly's "Frankie forgot his notebook and she didn't yell at *him*" with a judgment of his own, such as "Why are you worrying about Frankie? Just take care of your own responsibilities," chances are that Polly would have become even angrier. Dad's response worked because it was empathic and nonjudgmental. Polly came home furious with the teacher and would have ended up furious with her father had he not been so skillful.

Eleven-year-old Kim was something of a perfectionist. She had chosen a difficult piece to play for her piano recital and, after playing it poorly, she left the stage in tears. Backstage after the recital:

Mom: Don't cry. Everyone makes mistakes. I tried to tell you that piece was too advanced for you but you wouldn't listen to me.

Kim: Just leave me alone. I don't want to talk about it.

Kim's teacher took her aside: It's true, everyone does make mistakes but knowing that doesn't always help when you feel embarrassed and humiliated.

Kim: Well, I'm glad someone around here understands how I feel.

Both Mother and teacher were trying to make Kim feel better. Mother was trying to eliminate Kim's distress and it didn't work. The teacher's response did work because she accepted Kim's distress.

When Dad came home, Stuart greeted him with a long face:

Stuart: They chose parts for the play today.

Dad: The Greek play?

Stuart: Yes. I tried out for every part but the teacher let the kids vote on who should get each part and they voted by popularity, not by who was good. It's not fair.

Dad: *(wanting to murder Stuart's classmates for not choosing him)* You didn't get the part you wanted.

Stuart: *(tears brimming)* I didn't get any good part. I only got to be a Greek citizen with two crappy lines. It's not fair. I got up all my confidence to act and I tried out for every part.

Dad: *(tempted to say what a rat the teacher was for letting popularity be casting director, paused for a moment and said instead)* If you were the teacher, how would you choose?

Stuart: By talent. I'd choose the best actors.

Dad: You're angry that popularity determined the roles the kids got.

Stuart: Yeah, I don't even feel like going to the play and I was looking forward to it before today.

Dad: I can see why.

Stuart: *(grinning)* Oh, well, maybe I will go. We're all supposed to make this weird food to serve to the audience after the play.

Stuart's father was extremely skillful in responding to his son's humiliation and anger at getting only a minor role in the school play. Dad was just as angry with the teacher and classmates for hurting Stuart. All of us hate to see our children in pain, but Stuart's father didn't let his legitimate anger interfere with his ability to help Stuart at this trying moment. Nowhere did he attack the teacher, although he was furious with the teacher's unfairness. Father took care of Stuart's needs by carefully rephrasing his expressions ("You didn't get the part you wanted").

His statement, "You're angry that popularity determined the roles . . ." is an excellent example of the effectiveness of acknowledgment. By being sensitive to Stuart's emotions without denying them, minimizing their importance or sweeping them away, his father gave him just what he needed at that moment: true empathy.

When children complain about a teacher, neighbor, friend, camp counselor or bus driver, it is important not to side with the other person. Even a casual remark such as "how do you think the bus driver felt?" can make children think we are not taking their complaints seriously and do not believe them. Or they may feel that we care more about the other person than we do about them. It doesn't necessarily help to take the child's side either. If you feel a teacher is unjust, as Stuart's was, your criticism of the other person doesn't help the child who has to find ways of getting along with that other person every day.

Peter's parents have been divorced less than a year. He lives with his mother during the week and visits his father every weekend:

Peter: Daddy hardly ever gets to see me. I'm with you most of the time.

Mom: That's not true.

Peter: But I live with you every day and I only see Daddy on weekends.

Mom: If you sit down with me and look at the calendar, you'll see that you're with us equal amounts of time.

Peter: *(ignoring the calendar)* But Daddy doesn't get to see me at night. Daddy misses me.

Mom: That's not true. Daddy sees you Friday and Saturday nights.

Peter: But you have me Monday through Friday and Daddy only sees me Saturday and Sunday.

Mom: *(growing annoyed)* What do you do weekdays? I only see you in the morning before school and for a couple of hours in the evenings when we're too tired from being out all day. You and Daddy are together all Saturday and Sunday. You two get to relax and have fun together and we don't.

Peter said no more but continued to mope for the rest of the evening. Mother's denial of Peter's feelings is understandable. The situation is very painful for her and she obviously does not share Peter's feelings for her ex-husband. When Peter said, "Daddy hardly ever gets to see me. I'm with you most of the time," his words stabbed her. Peter didn't mean to attack her—he only missed his father. Any parent would be vulnerable in such a situation. It would be a rare parent who would not get defensive or feel hurt, and Peter's mother is not that rare parent. So her response was denial: "That's not true."

If feelings could be changed by rational arguments and objective facts, Peter would have been receptive to his mother's logic. She tried to reason with him and persuade him that he was wrong: "If you sit down with me and look at the calendar, you'll see that you're with us equal amounts of time." But to Peter, her words were irrelevant. He persisted in the hope of being heard. Had she been able to empathize with his longing to be with his father, she might have been able to say, "It sounds like you wish you could see Daddy more often."

Peter's mother didn't have to *do* anything. She didn't have to quit her job to spend more time with him. All he needed was her understanding of how much he missed his father. Although it is not easy to acknowledge children's feelings when our own emotions get in the way, if we are able to do so, we help them express and cope with their own distress.

Kirk's mother knew he dreaded an upcoming dermatologist's appointment. She hoped it would go smoothly.

Kirk: I don't feel like going to the skin doctor today.
Mom: I'm sure you don't.

Previously she would have said, "Don't worry. It won't be so bad." But now she was trying to acknowledge his feelings. At the doctor's office they were kept waiting over an hour.

Kirk: I'm really mad. He has no right to keep us waiting so long. I feel like leaving right now.
Mom: Yes, it is aggravating to have to wait this long. It doesn't seem fair.

A year earlier she remembered saying, "Be patient. The doctor is a very busy man." Finally they were ushered into the treatment room where a nurse was setting out ominous-looking implements.

Kirk: I don't like what I'm seeing.
Mom: They do look pretty formidable.

Mother watched the dermatologist work on Kirk's acne. Kirk winced a few times. When it was over, she touched his arm:

Mom: You really bore up well.
Kirk: That wasn't so bad. It only was bad when he pressed down.

By standing by him and reflecting his feelings rather than directing his behavior, she allowed Kirk to take control of his own problem.

Wendy's mother had been divorced since Wendy was five. She recently remarried, shortly after Wendy's eleventh birthday:

Wendy: Mom, I never get to spend any time with you since you married Scott.
Mom: Wendy, Scott and I stay home a lot more than we did before we got married. And you're always welcome to be with us.
Wendy: Yes, I know, but it's not the same as it was before.
Mom: Oh?
Wendy: Yes, I never get to be alone with just *you* anymore. We don't go skating together the way we used to.
Mom: It must be very hard for you to share me after just the two of us were together for so many years.
Wendy: I know I spend a lot of time with you and Scott, but not alone with just you.
Mom: I see. What do you think we could do about that?
Wendy: Maybe every night we could play a game or just be alone and talk?
Mom: What a good idea. On the nights when I'm home, we'll set aside a half hour of special time to be together.

A typical response to Wendy's words might be to interpret their meaning as anger about Scott's "intrusion" into Wendy's warm relationship with her mother. If her mother had drawn that conclusion, she probably would have become defensive.

But by listening carefully to Wendy, her mother realized that Wendy wasn't angry at Scott's presence—she just missed spending time alone with her mother.

Wendy's mother started out, as most of us would, by countering with facts ("Scott and I stay home a lot more than we did . . ."), but she quickly began to realize that Wendy needed more than facts. Mother did not know how to respond to Wendy's statement, "But it's not the same as it was before," so she bought some time by saying, "Oh?" This marvelous two-letter word ("Mmmmmm" works equally well!) can be a lifesaver when you do not know what to say. These "therapeutic grunts" not only buy you a few moments to think rather than answer on automatic, but they also are an understanding way of saying, "Yes, I hear you; please go on." They encourage a child to realize that we are listening, and to continue talking. They give us a chance to gain valuable information about what is bothering our child.

Beth: I hate myself.
Mom: Oh, Beth. What do you mean?
Beth: I really do.
Mom: I wonder what makes you feel that way.
Beth: I'm not pretty. I'm ugly.
Mom: What would a pretty girl look like?
Beth: She would have long hair.
Mom: And you don't.
Beth: No, you made me cut my hair for summer and now I look ugly.
Mom: You really wish you had long hair.

Beth nodded.

Mom: What can we do about it?
Beth: Not ever cut my hair again.
Mom: You want it to grow, and grow, and grow, and never cut it.

Beth: Not even trim it.
Mom: How long should we let it get?
Beth: Down to my shoulders.
Mom: And you could wear braids again. How would you feel then?
Beth: I'd really be pretty.

Beth's mood seemed to change as if by magic. But it was not magic—Beth's mother had become very skillful in acknowledging her daughter's feelings. By making the statement, "I wonder what makes you feel that way," she found a way of eliciting information. When children make negative statements about themselves such as "I hate myself . . . I'm dumb . . . Nobody likes me . . . ," a normal response is to contradict them immediately: "Of course, you don't hate yourself . . . You're not dumb; you're very smart . . . What do you mean? You have lots of friends . . ." Instead of contradicting Beth, her mother responded thoughtfully to discover the source of Beth's complaint with a brief, simple statement: "I wonder what makes you feel that way." Without probing directly, Beth's mother detected what was bothering Beth: "What would a pretty girl look like?" Had Beth's mother been on automatic, she might have given Beth ten reasons why short hair was practical for summer: "It's much cooler . . . it won't always be in your eyes when you swim . . ." Instead she responded to Beth's wish ("You really wish you had long hair") and she granted her wish in fantasy ("You want it to grow, and grow, and grow"). Beth's mother let the matter drop and bought herself some time to decide whether the length of Beth's hair was worth fighting about in the future.

When a child wants something we cannot or do not want to provide, we anticipate a head-on confrontation and often become angry with the child *just for wanting it*. Acknowledgment is difficult if we confuse feelings with behavior. A child's disappointment and anger because he can't have what he wants doesn't make him "bad." If you can only view the request as a *wish* that you have the right to deny, you can use acknowledgment to avoid a confrontation. ("Boy, you'd really like to have that," rather than, "Oh, God, you're never satisfied; you have so many toys already.") You can be permissive with feelings without being permissive with behavior. You can allow your children to want something without giving it to them and without feeling bad yourself for denying it. Sometimes your child will put up with not getting something because he feels satisfied enough by your acknowledgment that it is all right to want it.

Nell's father headed off a public blowup at a Chinese restaurant when he heard his five-year-old daughter's demands as ardent wishes and responded to them with lighthearted fantasy:

Dad: Let's order some Moo Shu pancakes. Two should be enough.
Nell: No, I want more.
Dad: How many should I order?
Nell: I want LOTS.
Dad: *(sensing a tantrum in the offing)* You like them so much. You really want a lot. How about fifty?
Nell: *(laughing)* No, a hundred.
Dad: One thousand!
Nell: The whole world!
Dad: Okay, the whole world of Moo Shu pancakes for Nell.

They laughed. When the waiter arrived, Dad ordered two Moo Shu pancakes and the rest of the meal was peaceful. By using fantasy instead of drawing up battle lines, Dad avoided the winner-loser game. A child who loses isn't an ideal dinner companion.

A downcast Michelle, six, walked across the playground toward her mother who sat, reading, on a park bench:

Michelle: Those big kids hurt my feelings. They said they could swing higher than me.

Mom: Why does that bother you? That's nothing to get upset about. They're bigger than you, that's all. I'm sure they didn't mean to hurt your feelings. Forget about swinging for now. Go and do something else. Play on the monkey bars or the seesaw.

Michelle sat next to her mother and sulked. Instead of going away and leaving Mother in peace, she repeatedly banged her shoes on the edge of the bench. Her mother's inability to "hear" her caused Michelle's sullen, provocative behavior.

Nicki's mother was more skillful. Nicki had been struggling with two different feelings. At four, she wanted to remain the family baby, but she also wanted to be a "big girl" like her seven-year-old sister. On Monday she would declare, "Everyone in this house thinks I'm a baby," and on Tuesday she would say indignantly, "I never want to grow up."

Nicki: I want to be a baby forever. I don't want to ever get older.

Mom: Forever? How old would you like to be?

Nicki: Ten years old.

Mom: *(about to contradict with* "But a baby isn't ten," *said instead)* What would you like to do when you're ten?

Nicki: I would like to just sit and blow bubbles all the time.

Mom: That sounds like fun. How big would the bubbles be?

Nicki: *(demonstrating with outstretched arms)* This big. And
        they'd float all the way up to the ceiling.

Mom and Nicki laughed. Had she been on automatic, Nicki's
mother would have tried to reason with Nicki ("Ten-year-
olds don't spend their time blowing bubbles . . ."). But by
letting Nicki's imagination roam freely and by mirroring Nicki's
wish to be grown up on the one hand and wanting to be
taken care of on the other, her mother let Nicki know that
she could accept her daughter's conflicting feelings. Like Nicki,
children often send us confusing, mixed messages.

We often assume that we understand what a child is thinking or feeling when perhaps we are off the mark. By replying
too fast, we may miss the chance to discover a child's real
meaning. When we are able to listen to children without
judging, criticizing or handing them a solution, we are often
surprised by what is actually troubling them, as Andrew was
when he took his four-year-old son, Matt, to the beach for
a vacation. As a child, Andrew had loved the ocean and often
told his son how much he had enjoyed swimming in the
waves, building sand castles and collecting shells. On the
first evening of their vacation, Matt adamantly refused to
sleep on the screened-in porch where Andrew had put his
sleeping bag. Matt insisted on sleeping in the room at the
back of the house, the one farthest from the ocean.

Dad: Why don't you want to sleep on the porch?
Matt: The ocean is too loud.
Dad: Matt, are you frightened of the ocean?
Matt: NO! It's just too loud.

Andrew decided to let Matt change rooms. As he was getting
ready for bed, Matt said, "I am a *little* scared of the ocean."

Dad: It's frightening?

Matt: Well, you know, when it rains there are a lot of waves. And they're very, very big.

Dad: That's true.

Matt: And they come all the time.

Dad: Mmmmm.

Matt: And then when you take a walk on the beach after the storm, all the shells are broken.

Andrew thought this was a fascinating revelation from a four-year-old. He wanted to make certain that he understood exactly what Matt meant so he repeated everything his son had said.

Dad: The shells do get broken. That's true, Matt. Sometimes the ocean can be dangerous.

Matt: Yes, Daddy.

Andrew tucked Matt in and kissed him good night. By listening to Matt carefully, his father discovered how differently children experience things and how rarely we adults can imagine their point of view.

When you acknowledge children's feelings, you needn't parrot their words verbatim. If that is all you do, children will quickly catch on and doubt your sincerity. There are a number of ways to be an empathic listener without sounding gimmicky:

You can paraphrase their words, as Andrew did when he replied to Matt's "I am a *little* scared . . ." with "It's frightening?" Sometimes a simple synonym is enough to keep our responses from sounding too mechanical.

You can also turn a child's statement into a question that invites more information than the harsh, interrogating "Why?" When Emily complained, "The teacher tore up my paper in front of the whole class," her mother acknowledged her distress by rephrasing it as a question: "She tore it up in front of everyone?" Mother needed more information. Sometimes we need to be detectives to learn what is bothering a child. When children make statements that we don't understand, repeating or rephrasing may be the best way to encourage them to give us more details. Or you can offer a non-judgmental brief reply, "Oh . . . I see . . . Un-huh . . . Mmmm . . ." that lets children know that you hear them and invites them to elaborate.

You can give their emotions a name. When her son described how classmates teased him about his new glasses, Barbara said, "You must have felt *embarrassed*." When her daughter complained that a friend had invited "everyone but me" to a skating party, Barbara responded, "I bet you feel *angry* and *disappointed* to be left out." Giving a name to children's feelings helps them clarify their emotions, feel understood and know that anger and embarrassment are normal and acceptable.

When acknowledging feelings is a new skill that we are trying to put into practice, we may be discouraged at a child's initial reaction. When Susan began to use the skill of acknowledgment, her ten-year-old daughter said, "Why are you talking to me like that?" because it was such a departure from Susan's usual way of responding. Older children may be especially suspicious when you begin to acknowledge their feelings because they may suspect you are trying to manipulate them, or they may question your sincerity.

When my son was going through a difficult period and came home each day with a new complaint about school, I used to respond with such judgmental remarks as "If you'd only try a little harder . . ." or "You'd better learn to get along with your teacher because you'll have her for the rest of the year." But when I became aware of the need to acknowledge his feelings, I tried to substitute empathic responses. When he said, "I hate school and my teacher is so unfair to me," the first time that I replied, "Gee, Eric, it sounds like you had a rough day," he looked at me with shock and hostility. Angrily he answered, "Stop being sarcastic." Then I realized that my taking his feelings seriously was so new that he misinterpreted it as sarcasm. His was a natural reaction to my sudden change of attitude.

When you try this approach you need to accept the fact that it will not always work miraculously. But if you continue to offer nonjudgmental acknowledgment, children will begin to recognize it as sincere empathy, not sarcasm or manipulation, and they will respond positively.

Acknowledgment is not always possible, nor is it always appropriate. Being a receptive listener takes time and energy, and there will obviously be many occasions when you cannot do it. If you come home after a frustrating day and are besieged at the door by three querulous children, you may need to take care of your own needs first. You might say, "Kids, I know you want me now, but I have to have fifteen minutes by myself. Let's set the timer; when it rings, you can knock on my door and then I'll be ready to listen to you." When both parent and child are in a state of turmoil, it's necessary to take care of the person who is most upset first. And that may often be the parent. Any attempt at true empathy is bound to backfire if you are harried, exhausted, preoccupied or anxious.

The skill of acknowledgment applies to feelings—not to misbehavior. When a child is using the living-room wall as a mural for his Magic Markers, empathy is not in order— clear limits are. This is not the time to say, "You wish you could use Magic Marker on the walls." This is the time to state firmly, "Markers are to be used *only* on paper. The wall must be cleaned immediately." If a child is walking on a high, wobbly fence, it is time to take action. It is not the time to say, "I bet you'd like to be a tightrope walker in the circus." It is time to say, "That is dangerous. Let me help you climb down so you won't get hurt." In both these situations, it is their behavior that you need to address, not their emotions.

In some situations we can set firm limits on children's behavior and then acknowledge their feelings. If Sandy is leaning into the crib and swatting the baby, her mother can say, "The baby is not to be hurt" and lift Sandy swiftly off the crib railing. Then she can deal with Sandy's emotions: "I see you're angry with your baby brother but hurting him isn't allowed."

There are other times when children do not want us to talk about their feelings; they want to be left alone. We can let them know that we are available without being intrusive:

Mom: You know that Dad and I are going to court to-
        morrow for the divorce settlement. How do you feel
        about it?
Jon: *(looking up from his comic book)* Okay.
Mom: Aren't you upset?
Jon: Not especially. I'll get to see Dad whenever I want.
Mom: Well, honey, if you do have a problem, I hope you'll
        come and talk to me about it.
Jon: Mom, do you love me?
Mom: You know I do!
Jon: Then, please, can I finish reading my comic?

Sometimes children want to be left in peace or to be alone with their feelings; they want to brood, not only over serious matters like divorce, but over little things. And they are entitled to that privacy.

As you develop the skill of acknowledgment, keep in mind that it is not a cure-all. We want to listen to children's troubles and be their allies but we cannot always "fix" their problems for them.

For some time Phyllis had realized that her eight-year-old son was anxious about not having a close friend. She wanted desperately to help him but she realized that there was little she could do other than offer to have his schoolmates visit. Perry's invitations to friends were rarely accepted and almost never reciprocated. On an evening when she was getting ready to go out, she found him sobbing on his bed:

Mom: Something is bothering you.

Perry: Uh-huh. *(He turned his face to the wall.)*

Mom: You seem pretty upset. Are you having a hard time with your composition? *(She had noticed his unfinished assignment on the floor beside his bed.)*

Perry: Yes, it makes me think of painful things.

Mom: Oh.

Perry: I want to tell you something but it's hard to say.

Mom: Some things are very tough to talk about.

Perry: It's only got seven words.

Mom: *(feeling the pressure of the clock and knowing that the sitter was due to arrive momentarily)* The dictionary is awfully big for me to find just the right seven words. I know some things are very hard to say.

Perry: Maybe I could write them down.

Mom: Okay, I'll get paper and a pencil.

Perry wrote: *"If only I had a close friend."*

Mom: I know how hard it is sometimes to make friends.

The sitter then arrived. Perry seemed to cheer up and was very outgoing with her. Though Mother said and did very little, she enabled Perry to express what was troubling him, which helped him cope. When Mother came home later, the sitter said Perry had finished his homework in just half an hour. The assignment had been to complete a composition that began, "John and Meg had known each other since nursery school. When they were in third grade, they sometimes played together but they were never good friends until early one winter morning when . . ."

Perry's mother read her son's composition; he had written an adventure that brought John and Meg together in lasting friendship. He had, in effect, made his own personal wish for a friend come true in the composition. Perry's misery was extremely painful to his mother but she did not reveal how distraught she was because he would have gotten the message that this was too serious a problem to overcome and he would have been further devastated. Phyllis neither sat in judgment nor offered criticism that would have made Perry feel that his lack of friends said something negative about him. ("What are you doing in school that makes kids not like you? . . . You must be doing something wrong . . .") Although Phyllis couldn't fix Perry's problem of having no friends, her quiet empathy enabled him to complete an assignment that had initially depressed and almost defeated him.

Sometimes a child becomes so upset that he wants to run away from home. The worst thing we can do in that case is to say, "I'll help you pack." Some parents think this "reverse psychology" is helpful, but it is not a caring response. It may send the child the message that we are indifferent to his leaving and, since he has nowhere else to go, that is the last thing he needs to hear. Drew's mother understood that no matter how angry or distraught a child is, he needs the reassurance that his parents want him no matter what:

Drew, eight: I want to run away! I want to be adopted by some other family.

Mom: You do?

Drew:	Yes, by another family where I'd be the only kid.
Mom:	You must be very unhappy with us if you want to run away.
Drew:	I AM! I hate Robbie and Jean. They're always making fun of me and teasing me. And you and Dad never tell them to shut up or punish them. You always take their side. I'm going to run away now.
Mom:	Oh, Drew, Daddy and I love you very much. And it would make us very, very sad if you left us. We would miss you too much.
Drew:	I'm going anyway.
Mom:	Well, I have bad news for you. I won't permit it! I wouldn't even allow you to be adopted by anyone else. I need you desperately. Who'd keep me company and be my welcome helper? *(Drew began to smile.)* And besides, who would take you? The ad would have to read: "A child with dirty nails, an untidy room and two pet snakes." I don't know, not too many takers.

Drew had now climbed into his mother's lap and was smiling.

It is painful to us as parents that we cannot straighten out all our children's dilemmas and ease all their suffering. When they are called names, picked last for the team, not invited to parties; when they're so distraught that they want to run away, there is little we can do—short of not making them feel worse about themselves. Our role is not to run after the child who is making ours so miserable and beat him up (though we may be tempted), or to blame our own child ("Well, what did you do first?"). Sometimes we need to accept that there is a limit to what we can do to protect children from hurtful situations. Often the only healer is time. What we *can* do for them is more important and immediate: by acknowledging their feelings, we can show children that we understand them, accept them and are on their side.

3

The Happiness Trap

Why It's Hard to Set Limits

All parents want their children to be happy, but that desire can sometimes prevent us from disciplining effectively. If our need to keep children happy and loving toward us is too compelling, we will find it impossible to say no to them.

Parents know they have to set limits to teach appropriate, acceptable behavior. But when they set limits, children are not pleased. They do not beam smiles at us and say, "Thanks so much for making me brush my teeth, pick up my toys, say 'please' and 'thank you,' share with my sister, be in bed by nine o'clock." Instead, they usually talk back to us, become angry or sulky, ignore us or outright defy us. Happy they are not.

At those times when we must discipline them firmly, they not only dislike our rules and requests, they dislike *us*. It is hard for children to separate what we do from who we are. When we insist that they do something they do not want to do or when we refuse to grant their requests, how often have we heard, "You're not my friend . . . I don't like you any-

more . . . You're mean . . . You don't love me . . . I hate
you . . ."

If we are out to win popularity contests with our children,
we're in trouble. We need to recognize and accept the fact
that children usually will be unhappy and will not like us
when we set limits. *At that moment* they dislike us but their
resentment is merely temporary.

Molly: Please, buy me some chewing gum.
Mom: No. Chewing gum is bad for your teeth.
Molly: I hate you.
Mom: You sound very angry.
Molly: Yes, and I don't love you anymore and I'll never
be your friend again.
Mom: You're angry enough to say you don't love me any-
more.
Molly: YES!
Mom: Maybe when you're not so angry, you'll feel like
loving me again.

Ten minutes later:

Molly: I'm not angry now. Will you play a game with me?
Mom: Sure, honey.

Molly's mother handled Molly's demand with great skill.
She anticipated that her denial of gum would upset Molly
but she did not take the "I hate you" personally. Many of
us might be devastated to be told by our child, "I don't love
you anymore," but Molly's mother knew this was a temporary feeling. When a child expresses intense dislike, or
even hatred toward us, it really says nothing about us as
parents; it merely says how strongly the child feels at that
moment. Molly's mother did not become defensive or feel
like a "bad mother" because of Molly's words—she did not
fall into the Happiness Trap. Instead, she stuck by the limit

(no chewing gum) and acknowledged Molly's feelings. She actually helped Molly clarify her anger and get over it by saying, "You're angry enough to say you don't love me . . . Maybe when you're not so angry, you'll feel like loving me again."

Children tend to catch on when we are concerned that saying "no" will make them unhappy and angry with us. It is difficult for them to accept limits when they know it is difficult for us to set them. Linda had this problem with her son who wore her down with the "sandpaper technique" and finally pulled her into the Happiness Trap:

David: I have to watch this program that's coming on next.
Linda: But you've watched TV since you got home from school this afternoon.
David: Yeah, but I don't have any homework tonight.
Linda: But, still . . .
David: Oh, come on, Mom, it's a great show.
Linda: But your eyes are looking glazed from so much television.
David: It's only a half-hour show.
Linda: But it's really a grown-up show. I don't think it's a good idea for you to be watching it . . .
David: All the other kids watch it every week. If you don't let me watch it, I'll be the only one who hasn't seen it.
Linda: Well . . . I suppose . . . Okay.

Linda caved in because she didn't want her son to be unhappy and didn't want him to be the only child in his crowd who hadn't viewed the program. Parents in our workshops frequently say that this argument—"but I'll be the only one"—traps them into relinquishing the limits. But a parent who recognized the Happiness Trap and was willing to risk his son's displeasure relayed this dialogue:

Paul: Please let me go with the kids to see the new movie that just opened in the mall.

Dad: That is not a movie for eight-year-olds.

Paul: That's not fair! All the kids are seeing it. You always treat me like a baby. Gregory's parents let him see it.

Dad: This movie is not for kids your age. If other people let their kids see it, that's their business. But I'm not comfortable with your seeing it, so the answer is no. If there is another movie you'd like to see, we can talk about it.

Another parent found that she was successful in banning violent television shows from her home because she had no ambivalence about saying, "In this house, we don't watch those programs." She explained, "We have few rules but the ones we have are absolute. The kids follow them because they know I have no shred of doubt about those rules. They are not up for negotiation." It's easier to set limits when the limit applies to a value you are trying to teach and when you are willing to risk a child's displeasure. When you are imparting a value such as honesty, no hitting or nonviolent television, you will have to adhere to the limits firmly. If you give in because you don't want an unhappy child, it will be difficult to communicate your values.

In many daily exchanges with children, a value may not even be involved. We may have difficulty setting limits on behavior simply because we have no particularly strong opinions about the issue at hand. We may be ambivalent in these situations because we're not sure how we feel about the issue or because we're unwilling to face a child's unhappiness if we say no. Barry's mother found herself in such a situation when they were on their way to his piano lesson and he begged her to stop at a street vendor's stand:

Barry: Can I have a hot dog first?

Mom: I don't think so.

Barry: Why not? Please! I'm starving.

Mom: No, I'm not feeling very well. It's cold and rainy and I don't feel like stopping.

Barry: Please, I really want one.

Mom: I know you want one, but please think of how I feel.

Barry: Okay, okay. But will you buy me a present instead?

Mom: Well . . . All right.

After his lesson, she bought candy as his present. Her indecisive answer, "I don't think so," encouraged his begging. She didn't have a strong view about whether or not he should have a hot dog and she was unwilling to give a firm no because she didn't want to see Barry upset so she replied with a weak plea ("I'm not feeling very well. It's cold and rainy . . .").

When Barry's mother replied to his third request with "I know you want one," she was on the right track. She acknowledged his wish. But unfortunately she jumped the track by talking about not feeling well. Had she added a simple "Not now" or "Not this afternoon," to the statement, "I know you want one," that would have been a clearer, more decisive no. Instead she tried to win his sympathy ("Please think of how I feel") because she did not want to grant his wish but she did not want to lose his affection either.

Her words implied that she owed him an apology for not buying a hot dog. By asking him to excuse her, she gave Barry too much power. He had the right to ask for a hot dog and she certainly had the right to refuse. Her eventual gift of candy, however, indicated that he *was* entitled to a reward for missing out on the hot dog.

When we mean "no," we need to say it decisively. If there is a "maybe" in our tone of voice, a child will instantly detect that soft spot and zero in on it. If you are unsure of how to reply to a child's demand, you can always buy some time with an answer like "Let me think about that. I'll tell you fifteen minutes from now." Or you can count to ten before answering, which often helps avoid lengthy arguments. Of course there are some children whose fighting spirit becomes activated by the sound of the word "no" and will try to wear us down with endless arguments. All the more reason to decide, before we utter the word "no," what is a non-negotiable issue and to be prepared to follow through.

Children sometimes try to catch us in the Happiness Trap by pinning the "bad parent" label on us. Keith's mother could have become hurt and defensive at his provocative remarks when he inspected the refrigerator and pronounced her an inept parent. But she did not:

Keith: There's never anything good to eat around here.
Mom: I'm sure you can find something.
Keith: There's nothing here that doesn't have to be heated up. This kitchen is practically empty. It's like we're poor.

Mom was tempted to impart a lesson on famine in Africa but she refrained.

Mom: How about an apple or a tangerine?
Keith: Ugh! Disgusting.
Mom: Well, you're pretty resourceful. I'll bet if you look around, you'll find something you like.
Keith: You are my mother and it's your responsibility to see that there's decent food in this house.

With enormous restraint, she said nothing and walked out of the kitchen. Keith eventually found some crackers and spread them with peanut butter.

Had she let herself be vulnerable to the "bad mother" accusations, she would have tried to justify her actions ("I was too busy to get to the market today") or lectured ("You never want what's good for you; all you want is junk food"), but she knew such remarks would only ignite an argument. Exiting from the scene was the most effective way to deal with his hostility at that moment.* She did not feel guilty about having a sparse larder; she did not drop everything and run to the store for bags of cookies and potato chips. Nor did she reach for her wallet so that he could go to the corner store himself. She was able to accept his unhappiness about the culinary choices available just then and recognize that it said nothing negative about her.

Lisa was much younger than Keith. She too tried accusation when she wanted to maneuver her father into reading extra bedtime stories, but Dad didn't let himself be manipulated:

Lisa: Daddy, read me these stories.
Dad: Three stories are too many. I'm very tired tonight.
Lisa: You're mean. I'm three so I get three stories. When I'm four, you'll have to read me four.
Dad: You'd like three stories, but not tonight.
Lisa: Mommy would read me three.
Daddy: I hear how much you want me to read to you. You'd like it if I could read ten stories, but tonight I am reading only one. You may choose between *Curious George* or *Goodnight Moon*.
Lisa: Okay, *Goodnight Moon*.

Dad stuck to the limit he wanted to set. It was easier for Lisa to accept his limit because he gave her a choice.

To Theo, four, the local transit museum was pure heaven. He had visited it a dozen times and never grew tired of its locomotives and trolleys.

*See Chapter 5 for more about exiting and handling our own anger.

Theo: I want to go to the transit museum today, Mommy.
Mom: Not today.
Theo: I want to go TODAY.
Mom: We went a few days ago. I don't want to go today. Maybe Daddy will take you soon.
Theo: I'm GOING to the transit museum.
Mom: I hear you. You're disappointed and angry.
Theo: *(kicking the furniture)* I'M GOING!
Mom: Kicking the furniture is not allowed. *(And she paused a moment.)* You're really furious. It's okay to be angry. I don't blame you. I bet you wish I were the kind of mommy who would take you to the transit museum every day, but I'm not.
Theo: *(sobbing)* I wanted to go today. Can we go tomorrow?
Mom: *(putting her arms around him)* Let me think about that. We certainly will go again soon.

Theo's mother began this dialogue on a weak note when she tried to change his mind by explanation. "We went a few days ago. I don't want to go today" were irrelevant to Theo so he tuned her out by replying: "I'M GOING . . ."

Why don't explanations work? Because we often give children explanations in an attempt to change their minds and make them agree with us. We hope they'll buy the explanation and not be angry with us. But after a thousand explanations, children still want what they want as much as they wanted it before. And we just have to deal with not giving them what they want.

As soon as Theo's mother realized that her explanations were useless, she tried something more effective. She acknowledged how he was feeling: "I hear you. You're disappointed and angry." She simultaneously remained resolute ("Kicking the furniture is not allowed"), reflected his emotions and let him know that it was all right to be angry. Because she was comfortable with setting a limit, she was able to empathize with his anger. Her statement, "I bet you wish I were the kind of mommy who would take you to the transit museum every day, but I'm not" was kind, but there was nothing apologetic about it. That statement was a caring and convincing way to teach Theo that even when he wants something dearly, Mother will not always grant it—yet it is perfectly acceptable to want it. She did not blame or criticize him for wanting to go to the transit museum every day, but neither did she blame herself for denying his wish and making him unhappy. She respected her own limits.

When children say, "You're mean . . . You don't love me . . . You're not fair . . ." and other angry retorts because they do not want to accept limits, some parents may be tempted to agree: "Well, perhaps I am being too harsh . . . maybe if I had more patience . . . if only I could spend more time with him, he might not be so cranky . . ." These guilt-tainted feelings, coupled with the need to keep our children happy and loving toward us, can melt our attempts to discipline effectively. Several parents have expressed the experience of falling into the Happiness Trap and being overwhelmed by feelings of guilt and failure: "When she's mad at me I somehow feel I've blown it." . . . "I feel like a good parent when she's happy and a bad parent when she's not. . . ."

Lorraine was hardly a negligent mother. She enjoyed her job and needed the income. Even though her husband was at home with their daughter in the evenings, Lorraine worried about working long hours and not spending enough time with Heather. Like a five-year-old judge in black robes, Heather picked up on her mother's guilt and pronounced the verdict: unfit mother. One evening when she could not arrive home until eight, Lorraine said, "I already felt guilty about being so late and I expected Heather to be extra angry. As soon as

I came through the door, she yelled, 'I don't want to see you anymore. And I don't want to talk to you anymore.' The scene was like many we've had lately—she, full of anger, and me, full of remorse."

In our workshops Lorraine became aware of her ambivalence about working and learned to respond to Heather's accusatory words in a new way. On a Sunday morning they were baking muffins together:

Heather: Annie's mommy is a real good cook. She doesn't go to work.
Mom: Is she?
Heather: She cooks a lot. She always makes special snacks for us after school.
Mom: *(still not falling for it)* I like special snacks, too.

(Courtesy of Jan Eliot)

Heather: Well, *her* mommy makes us popcorn and cup-
           cakes and stuff like that all the time.
Mom: Really?
Heather: She goes to work but she's always home when
           Annie comes home from school.

At this point Lorraine could not resist bringing in a bit of
reality.

Mom: I think Annie's mother works at home, doing
           housework and things.
Heather: No, no. She works business work like you, only
           she comes home to be with Annie after school.
Mom: You wish I could be home every afternoon like
           Annie's mother. I know. Hey, did you ever taste
           banana muffins like these?
Heather: They're not muffins yet. They're batter.
Mom: To me the batter tastes as good as muffins.

Lorraine stuck her finger in the bowl of batter and licked a
large dollop. Heather followed her example, giggled and said,
"Oooh, I like this too."

Mom: (*laughing*) If we eat all the batter, there won't be
           any muffins.

As soon as she gave up explaining why she had to work
and could not be home "like Annie's mother," Lorraine no
longer acted like a "depriving working mother" and didn't
allow Heather to play on her guilt. Just as we try not to sit
in judgment of our children, we must not allow them to sit
in judgment of us.

Stephanie, too, held a demanding job and had limited time
with her two children. When she was with them she was
warm and responsive and gave them her undivided attention.
She had just finished playing two games of Candyland with

her four-year-old daughter and Deena was bargaining for a third:

Deena: Please, Mommy, one more game.
Mom: No, that's enough for now. It's time for dinner.
Deena: *(lower lip quivering)* You're making me unhappy. You're going to make me cry.

Stephanie was about to give in when she realized she was falling into the Happiness Trap. "Wait a minute," she said to herself, "just because I've been at the office all day and was in Detroit part of last week, that doesn't mean I have to play three games of Candyland to prove I'm a good mother."

Mom: Two games are enough for now, honey. Maybe we could play another game tomorrow. But I could use some help in the kitchen now.

Seeing her mother standing firm, Deena picked up the cards, folded the game board and said, "Okay, but I bet I win the next time."

Stephanie spoke at length about her guilt feelings: "I used to wonder if I did enough for my children. Every time I said, 'Enough is enough,' and put my foot down, I felt those familiar pangs. But I had to realize that nobody can be Supermom. I have needs, too, and I can't always take care of their needs ahead of mine."

This awareness became apparent a few weeks later when Stephanie and her husband were in a black mood. They had just learned that they would be unable to buy a house that they had bid on. All through dinner, they tried to suppress their gloom while Deena babbled on. By bedtime, Deena was a fountain of demands, insisting on juice in a special thermos, having her dolls arranged in a certain order and staying up an hour later. Stephanie was about to explode, as most of us would at this point, and attack her daughter by shouting, "Listen, brat, you're not the only one around here with needs." Instead, she responded to Deena with a statement of her own limitations: "Deena, probably you don't know it, but Mommy is very upset tonight. It has nothing to do with you, but I need to be left alone right now. Here's a hug and a kiss. I'll see you in the morning."

As she spoke, Stephanie said later, she felt the familiar pull of guilt: "There was a part of me that said, 'You know, she's your daughter and she needs your attention even though you feel rotten.'" But Stephanie did not let her daughter know how guilty she felt. She neither blamed herself for being temporarily unavailable, nor blamed Deena for making demands that she could not meet. Rather, she stated her feelings eloquently, saying in effect, "Mommy can only do so much."

Darren's mother, Louise, shows how we can be loving yet firm disciplinarians once we free ourselves from the Happiness Trap. Louise and six-year-old Darren stayed up late watching a movie on their VCR:

Darren: Please, Mom, can't we watch it again?

Mom: Well, Darren, I'm not too sure. . . . It's pretty late.

Darren: Aw, come on, Mom, it was so good. It's not that long.

Mom: It's too late. It's time for bed.

Darren: *(sobbing)* I wanted to watch it once more. If you don't let me, I'm never going to do anything for you again. When you ask me for something, I'm going to say, "NO!" If you ask me for a hug, I won't give it to you. Then you'll see how it feels.

Mom: Darren, I understand that you're hurt that you didn't get your way and I'm sorry about that. It's hard to hear 'no' and accept it. I understand.

Darren: I really liked that movie. I wish I could see it again.

Mom: Yes, Darren, I know. I wish it were earlier so we could. I liked it, too. But now it is bedtime.

At first Louise gave an indecisive answer, ". . . I'm not too sure . . ." so Darren saw an opening to beg and cajole. As she spoke those words, Louise saw that she was getting herself into a box. When she realized this, she was able to set a clear limit ("It's time for bed") and then acknowledge Darren's disappointment ("I understand that you're hurt . . ."). "It's hard to hear 'no' and accept it . . ." was an empathic statement that is hard to make when you feel guilty or defensive.

If you can put aside your constant need to be loved, you will be able to set limits and give yourself permission to say "no." You can also give your children permission to be angry, disappointed, grumpy or even hostile. Once you spring yourself from the Happiness Trap, you can acknowledge your child's feelings and still teach appropriate behavior. But this does not mean you will have a happy child who will say, "Thanks for saying 'no,' Mom. I really respect your limits."

4

Why Punishment Doesn't Work and What Does

Even when we do set firm limits, we are at some point faced with a child's exceeding them and breaking our rules. What then? Most of us resort to the only disciplinary tool we know: punishment.

All afternoon nine-year-old Todd bugged his father to let him spend the night at a friend's house. Todd refused to take "no" for an answer:

Dad: You know you're not allowed to sleep over on a school night.

Todd: But we'll go to bed early. I promise.

Dad: Todd, you know the rule. The subject is closed. Now drop it.

Todd: You mean, stupid jerk.

Dad: (*yelling*) That's it! Now you're going to be punished. Get to your room! And stay there. There'll be no TV for two weeks.

Todd ran to his room, slammed the door and scrawled furiously all over his walls—fortunately with chalk—BULLY! BULLY! BULLY! MY FATHER IS A BULLY!

Did this punishment work? Did it correct Todd's obnoxious behavior? Clearly not. Todd responded to his punishment with rage at his father. He did not go to his room and quietly contemplate his transgressions. Todd did no emotional homework. He didn't say to himself, "Gee, Dad was right. I was pretty awful. I deserve to be punished." Instead he focused all his energy on getting back at his father—and he did so in a most graphic manner.

The problem with punishment is that we usually dish it out in a punitive, hurtful spirit. When a child's behavior angers or hurts us, it is difficult not to be punitive. But when we punish in an impulsive desire to get even with a child, we are ineffective in changing his behavior. Children respond to our wish for vengeance by concentrating on retaliation, not on their own misdeeds.

To punish means "to inflict injury on, hurt, impose a penalty, cause loss or pain." Anyone—child or adult—reacts to injury, pain or hurt with rage and defiance. We want to strike back, as Todd did. We become full of resentment or go out of our way to avoid the punisher:

Mom: It's bedtime, Fred. Time for lights-out.

Fred: Mommy, I want to read the bear book.

Mom: It's too late.

Fred: But, Mom . . .

Dad: Fred, that's it! No book. Under the covers. No pouting. One more sound out of you and you'll get a spanking.

Dad left the room.

Fred: I *hate* Daddy. He's not the boss. He's mean. I HATE, HATE, HATE him. When I'm bigger I'm going to tell *him* what to do. I wish he'd divorce and I could trade him. I know! I won't let him divorce. Just the next time he tries to boss me, I won't let him have any hugs or kisses. Then he'll be sorry.

His father's threatened punishment ("One more sound out of you and you'll get a spanking") didn't encourage Fred's cooperation in turning out the light and going to sleep. Instead his punitive words made four-year-old Fred so resentful and angry that he wanted to punish his father back. What could Dad have done? He could have acknowledged Fred's wish: "I know you like the bear book. Maybe tomorrow night we can start earlier and I can read it to you" and still set the limit: "But now I'm turning out the light," instead of threatening to spank him.

Ten-year-old Mimi had left a pile of books, games and clothes in the hall outside her room:

Mom: Please put all this stuff away.
Mimi: I'll do it later.
Mom: Later is your favorite word. I want you to do it now.
Mimi: Mom, I'm watching a great show. I'll do it when this program is over.

The show ended, another began and Mimi didn't move.

Mom: Now I'm really mad. You said you'd do it. If this mess isn't cleaned up this minute, I'll punish you.
Mimi: I'm too tired. I'll do it tomorrow.
Mom: No! Tomorrow is not soon enough.
Mimi: You can't make me.
Mom: Okay, if you don't put these things away now, you'll get no allowance.
Mimi: I don't care. I'll get it from Daddy this weekend.

Mimi's mother threatened to punish her by taking away her allowance because she was understandably at the end of her rope. But punishment—and threats of punishment—often boomerang in a show of indifference or defiance from a child ("I don't care. I'll get it from Daddy . . .") and we are left feeling more angry and helpless. Punishment becomes a vicious cycle. As soon as you say, "I'm going to punish you . . ." a red flag shoots up before children's eyes. Like Mimi, they instantly take a defensive posture and retort with those all-too-familiar phrases: "You can't make me . . . I don't care . . . So what? . . . I didn't want to watch TV anyway . . ."

Every time Hugh's parents punished him by depriving him of TV, movies or weekend outings, he had a delayed reaction. Earlier in the day, Hugh had been punished for talking back. When his parents were about to leave for the evening:

Mom: I want you to be a good boy tonight and not do anything wrong. I don't want to come home and get a bad report from the sitter.

Hugh: Okay, Mommy.

As soon as they left, the sitter later reported, seven-year-old Hugh went on a rampage, running through the house, pushing every button on every appliance. He turned on the air conditioner, TV, electric stove, dishwasher, hi-fi, radio, toaster . . . The sitter ran after him, turning everything off. He then proceeded to throw one of his toys out the window. When his mother first came to my workshop, she said this behavior was habitual with Hugh; if she punished him in the morning he waited until their next evening out to begin his button-pushing cycle again.

"He'd drive the baby-sitter crazy," Hugh's mother said. "And the next morning, I'd be infuriated. It was like he was paying us back by doing everything he knew we didn't want him to do." Punishment often leads our children to be imaginative in the arena that is least constructive for them or for us: revenge.

Punishment can also make a child more careful in committing an offense or sneaky about concealing it. Children who are frequently punished often become more devious, not more honest or responsible. Anita exceeded her Halloween candy limit, so her mother punished her by taking away her trick-or-treat bag. Two days later, when Mother was changing the linens, she found a stash of candy wrappers tucked inside Anita's pillowcase.

Parents in my workshops often recall from childhood how ineffective punishment was—they were spanked, sent to their rooms, deprived of precious possessions. They vividly remember those punishments but they rarely remember what they did to "deserve" them.

Margaret had never forgotten her father's standard operating punishment: "He used to give me a thump on the head. A few weeks ago, he was with us when my son was acting up. Dad said, 'Why don't you thump him on the head?' Just the idea was horrible to me. I always remember how demeaning it was. When he said that, all those old feelings of humiliation welled up in me and I wanted to say, 'How dare you even suggest it!' And I don't even remember what he did the head thumping for!"

Sometimes you may strike your children in exasperation "to teach them a lesson." But what lesson are they learning? When you're angry, hit. After we hit children, we are uncomfortable and guilt-ridden. I think this guilt is appropriate—the fact is, hitting hurts. Sometimes we are so enraged that we can't stop ourselves. That is part of being human. But it is an illusion to justify hitting as a form of positive discipline. And if we hit our children when *we* are angry, it's going to be very difficult to prevent them from hitting us, a sibling or a playmate when *they* are angry.

Some children seek punishment to relieve their guilt. They want to wipe the slate clean so they can misbehave again. Selma Fraiberg, author of *The Magic Years*, called this a "bookkeeping approach to misconduct." She wrote:

A child may learn how to avoid successfully any guilt feeling for bad behavior by setting up a cycle in which the punishment cancels the "crime" and the child, having paid for his mischief, is free to repeat the act another time without the attendant guilt feelings. Some children have an elaborate accounting system which permits them to go into debt on the "sin" side of the ledger up to a certain amount and pay off periodically on the punishment side by getting themselves spanked.*

Do we want children to become little accountants, balancing their crimes and punishments? A child without guilt is a child without a conscience. Guilt is often an appropriate response to wrongdoing, but punishment impedes the development of a conscience by taking away the opportunity for him to feel guilty. He has no chance to develop inner motivation.

When eleven-year-old Pete broke a piece of sculpture that his father had spent hours crafting, his father was terribly upset. He found Pete carefully trying to piece it back together:

Dad: I'm furious. That sculpture meant a lot to me and now it's ruined.
Pete: I'm really sorry, Dad. You can have my allowance to buy more clay for another sculpture.
Dad: Yes, Pete. That would be a good idea.

Angry as he was, Pete's father did not give in to the temptation to punish him because he realized that Pete was trying to make amends. By *not* punishing, he let Pete be contrite and take responsibility for his action. Remorse couldn't fix the sculpture, but neither would a spanking.

*Selma Fraiberg, *The Magic Years* (New York: Charles Scribner's Sons, 1959), pp. 253–54.

What Does Work?

Our goals are to help children understand what is and what is not appropriate behavior, to help them correct misbehavior and learn not to repeat it. Instead of being punitive, you can teach acceptable conduct by using alternatives to punishment:

—You can help your children find solutions and let them be part of the problem-solving process.

—You can diminish the need to punish by letting appropriate consequences be the teacher.

—You can let them know of your feelings of anger or disappointment and give them a chance to make amends. (See Chapter 5.)

Andy's teacher called to say that he had been misbehaving on the school bus. Andy's father had learned that punishing Andy, eight, only backfired so he put Andy in the position of problem solver:

Dad: Andy, I have something very serious to talk to you about.

Andy: What?

Dad: We have a problem. The school called and told me that you were acting wild on the bus, not listening to the driver and being disrespectful. They said you might have to go to the principal's office and might not be allowed to ride the bus for a while.

Andy: *(teary)* I'm not the only one.

Dad: I'm sure that's true, but you are my child and I love you and I don't want to see you in trouble. I know it's hard because you have so much fun with your friends on the bus. But I think you need to solve this problem. What do you think you can do?

Andy: Well . . . I could sit up front, near the driver, and not with the wilder guys.
Dad: That's a good idea.

The next day, Andy's father walked with him to the bus stop and told the driver that Andy would be sitting next to him for a while. There were no more calls from the school about Andy's bus behavior. Had Andy not found his own solution, his father could have offered him some choices: "Would you rather ride your bike to school or sit apart from your friends on the bus?"

When the teacher first called, Dad's initial reaction was to punish Andy but he thought instead about what he would say to his son. He actually helped Andy *avoid* a serious punishment (expulsion from the bus) by being solution-oriented. He supported Andy ("I'm sure that's true") and offered Andy a nonpunitive option ("What do you think you can do?"). Andy's father helped motivate his son to change his behavior rather than eliciting his defiance.

By inviting our children's solutions rather than delivering an impulsive punishment, we can often gain information about what is troubling them, as Betsy's mother did:

Mom: Betsy, it's time to go to the hairdresser.
Betsy: I don't want to go. I don't feel good.
Mom: Going to the hairdresser makes you feel crummy?
Betsy: Yeah, I'm sick. I'm not going.
Mom: Betsy, I hear that you don't want to go, but we both have appointments which we must keep. How can I help make this easier for you?
Betsy: I only want my hair cut. No shampoo.
Mom: The shampoo bothers you in some way?
Betsy: Yes. He pulled my hair out the last time.
Mom: He pulled hard and hurt you, and maybe you're scared it will hurt again?

Betsy: Yes. I'll go and have my hair cut, but no shampoo.

Mom: We'll go for the cut and I'll talk to him about the shampoo problem.

This incident could have become a major power struggle with Betsy refusing to budge and Mom threatening to drag her forcibly to the hairdresser. But instead of making a punitive statement like, "You can forget about going to the circus on Saturday if you won't come now," her mother listened sympathetically ("How can I help make this easier for you?") and drew out the real reason Betsy refused to go to the hairdresser. Betsy's mother was able to engage Betsy's cooperation in solving the problem because she took time to gain information.

Ivan's parents were away for the weekend and his grandmother was baby-sitting. When they got home, Grandma told his parents that Ivan, six, had taken his mother's best perfume—not the first time he had done so—and sprayed it all over the cat. His parents raised the issue with him after Grandma left:

Dad: I understand you played with Mommy's perfume. Is this true?

Ivan: Yes.

Dad: I'm pleased you told me the truth, but I'm very disappointed. You promised that you would not do this ever again. This makes me very angry.

Ivan: I'm sorry.

Mom: Daddy and I are very upset. We don't know what to do about this. What do you think should be done?

Ivan: Punish me?

Dad: I don't think punishment will solve anything.

Mom: Well, maybe we should put a lock on the door to keep you out of our room.

Ivan: *(pauses)* Yes, I want you to.

Mom: What?
Ivan: Yes, put a lock on the door.
Mom: Okay, perhaps we will.

Dad first responded by praising Ivan for telling the truth. Without sounding punitive, he clearly stated how disturbed he was by Ivan's action. Ivan's apology demonstrates how much children care about how parents feel. If his parents had ranted and raved and punished him, Ivan would not have been given the opportunity to feel contrite and to say, "I'm sorry."

When his mother asked, "What do you think should be done?" Ivan offered, "Punish me?" because, as Selma Fraiberg said, children sometimes seek punishment as a way of relieving guilt.

Ivan was asking his parents' help in curbing his impulsive behavior. For a young child like Ivan, impulses are often too strong to resist. When he agreed to a lock on the door—to his mother's amazement—he was saying, in effect, "The temptation to spray the cat with perfume is too great, so a lock would help me."

Consequences are another alternative to punishment. The contrast between the following two examples shows how much more effectively consequences teach than punishment.

Scott, five, ran to the elevator with his friend Sheri who had been visiting for the day. He charged ahead of her.

Scott: I win. I get to push the button.
Sheri: No fair. I want to do it.
Scott's mother: Scott, give Sheri a turn to ring. She is our guest.

Scott pushed the button again.

Sheri: It was my turn and he pushed it anyway.

Mom:	*(angrily)* Scott, I told you not to push that button. It was Sheri's turn. You're a very bad boy.
Scott:	*(holding his hand over the button)* Well, I was just sharing the bell with her.
Mom:	You're a liar, Scott. You rang just to be mean and selfish. Why don't you *ever* do what I tell you? I'm going to give you a spanking for this!

She grabbed Scott and spanked him in front of Sheri and her mother while apologizing to them for his freshness. For the rest of the day, whenever he looked at his mother, Scott "shot" her by using his hand as a pretend gun. He muttered about ways to get rid of her and grumbled, "Nobody likes me."

What did Scott's mother do? She reacted punitively. She was angry and embarrassed because he had misbehaved in front of Sheri's mother. She labeled him a liar, bad, mean and selfish. She took Sheri's side twice which made Scott more defiant, and then she humiliated him by hitting him in the presence of a friend.

Another mother handled a similar conflict quite differently. After finding that punishment usually backfired with her four-year-old daughter, she began to substitute consequences:

Pam and Jody had been playing at Jody's house while their mothers chatted in the kitchen. Pam hit Jody.

Pam's mom:	Hitting is not allowed. If you hit Jody again, we will have to go home.
Pam:	I won't, Mommy.

Twenty minutes later, she hit Jody again.

Mom: *(calmly)* We will have to go now.

Pam began to cry.

Mom: I can see that you're sad about leaving.
Pam: I want to stay and play.
Mom: I know, but we will have to leave now. Would
                  you like to make a date for next week?
Pam: Yes.

The mothers agreed on next Thursday. Pam cried on the way home but her mother refrained from lecturing or scolding ("If you hadn't been so mean to her, you'd still be playing with her now"). Such statements are tempting, but Pam's mother knew that when children are upset, they are not amenable to reasoning. She responded to Pam's tears with silence and allowed her daughter to experience sadness, the consequence of having to leave. When they arrived home:

Pam: Why did we have to leave?
Mom: Why do you think we had to leave?
Pam: Because I hit Jody.
Mom: That's right.

At bedtime, Pam brought up the subject again:

Pam: Tell me what happened when I was at Jody's.
Mom: What should I tell you?
Pam: Why I was sad.
Mom: Because we had to leave.
Pam: I hit Jody. I wanted to stay for a snack.
Mom: Next time, maybe we will be able to.

As a result of her mother's skillful responses, Pam clearly understood her misbehavior and its consequences ("Why do you think we had to leave?" "Because I hit Jody"). This conflict was successfully resolved because Pam's mother first set a limit ("If you hit Jody again, we will have to go home"), then followed through authoritatively. She expressed confidence in her daughter by giving her another chance ("Next time, maybe we will be able to"). When using consequences, it is important not to add punitive statements like "This will teach you" or "It serves you right." If Pam's mother had said, "I warned you. You got what you deserved," Pam would have experienced this as a punishment, not as an appropriate opportunity to learn that hitting is unacceptable and has undesirable consequences. This doesn't mean that Pam will never hit another child again, but if it eliminates hitting at just a few play sessions, Pam has begun to learn more appropriate behavior.

For Christmas, eight-year-old David received a special toboggan with a bright yellow steering wheel and ski-like runners from his grandmother. He took it into the yard and sat on it, practicing for an inevitable snowstorm. When rain began to fall two days after Christmas, his mother suggested that he bring it inside "so it won't rust." David said he would, but didn't. When snow finally fell a week later, the toboggan was missing. David looked all over the yard. No one had brought it inside. It could only have been stolen.

David was heartbroken: "It was my favorite present and I didn't even get to use it in the snow!" he cried. His mother's initial reaction was to speak punitively ("It was your responsibility. I told you to bring it in. Now you've lost an expensive present and you're going to be punished"). If she had added punishment to his loss, he would undoubtedly have been angry with her rather than sad about losing the toboggan, and a "lesson" about leaving anything precious outside would have been lost. When he asked if he could get another toboggan, she simply replied, "no," without delivering a lecture.

Gary's father also let consequences teach in a difficult situation:

Dad:	Gary, Uncle Jack called late last night because he got back to his apartment and couldn't find his keys. He was locked out and had to stay at a neighbor's. He said he had the keys when he was here yesterday afternoon.
Gary, five:	Uh-huh.
Dad:	I found his keys this morning in the bottom of our umbrella stand. Do you know how they got there?
Gary:	No, I didn't take them.
Dad:	Gary, are you afraid to tell me the truth because you're afraid I'll punish you?
Gary:	Well . . . sort of.
Dad:	I might get angry, but I'd rather you tell me the truth so we can work out this problem.
Gary:	Well, I was playing with Uncle Jack and I thought I'd just hide the keys and . . . I don't know.
Dad:	I'm glad you admitted you hid the keys, but I want you to think of how Uncle Jack felt when he got home at midnight and couldn't get in because he had no key. That was very upsetting to him and it was an imposition on his neighbor. Jack had to wake him up in the middle of the night.

Gary began to cry. Jack was his favorite uncle and the thought of causing him distress made Gary truly contrite. He called Uncle Jack to apologize and said he and his father would bring the keys right over.

Instead of accusing Gary or punishing him, his father first described the situation in order to give his son the opportunity to explain the mystery of the missing keys. When Gary denied taking them ("No, I didn't take them"), Gary's father dealt with the honesty issue in a forthright manner by asking, ". . . are you afraid to tell me the truth because you're afraid I'll punish you?" His father fortunately didn't press him with an inquisitory "You hid them, didn't you?" Too often an accusatory remark like that causes children to lie, especially if they feel it is not safe to tell the truth. Gary's father made it safe by saying, "I might get angry, but I'd rather you tell me the truth so we can work out this problem," thus making it easier for Gary to admit hiding the keys. By involving Gary emotionally in the consequences of his playful but irresponsible action, his father helped Gary think about right and wrong.

The quickest way to get a child to lie is to ask a question when you already know the answer. The child will sense the trap and choose a lie to avoid getting caught. Children think, "Why tell the truth if I'm going to be blamed or punished?" No one wants to incriminate himself.

Monique's teacher called to say that Monique had not turned in any math homework all week:

Mother: How are you doing in math?
Monique: Okay.

Her mother's incriminating question was a trap. Monique felt cornered, so her answer was a vague lie because she expected her mother to yell or punish her if she told the truth. Another parent handled the same situation directly, by describing the problem factually: "The teacher called. There seems to be a problem with your homework. We need to discuss it, so we can figure out a way to fix it."

Sometimes parents punish children by depriving them of a privilege, allowance or favorite toy. Such deprivations are easy to inflict: "No bedtime story for you tonight . . . I'm taking away your new skateboard for a month . . . No more staying up late on weekends . . ." But these are not always appropriate consequences to the child's misbehavior. *Appropriate* is the key here. Consequences that are relevant, that flow from a child's action, make sense to a child and can truly teach. But arbitrary consequences do not help a child reflect on what she has done wrong. For instance, when Mom deprived three-year-old Connie of her beloved teddy bear because Connie had been playing with her food, Connie focused only on losing Teddy. It didn't stop her from playing with her food at the next meal because there was no connection between her behavior and her punishment. A more appropriate consequence would have been simply to remove Connie from the table.

When Ricky continued to ride his bike after he had repeatedly been called to dinner, his parents said, "You can't ride your bike after dinner because you did not stop riding when we called you." That is an appropriate consequence to his behavior, a logical result of his disobedience. But if they had taken his bike away for punching his sister, it would have been an inappropriate consequence. Sometimes it is hard to find an appropriate consequence, especially in the middle of a battle, which is why we need to distance ourselves whenever possible before we impose consequences.

Parents who are new to this approach of substituting solutions or consequences for punishment sometimes say, "But when my child gets totally out of control or throws a temper tantrum, I just have to spank him or take away his favorite toy to teach him that he can't get away with that behavior." When a child is in the throes of a temper tantrum, however, such punishment will only increase his frenzy. Sometimes the most helpful response to a tantrum is to say firmly, "We can deal with this when you've calmed down. Right now we need to be apart. When you're ready to talk in a way that I can understand, I'll be in the next room." Sometimes by staying and trying to reason with him, we just add fuel to his tantrum. We may even have a tantrum of our own. Of course, there is no single "right" way to respond when a child loses control. Being left alone may not be the treatment of choice for certain children who may become more hysterical and need the steadying presence of an adult; in that case, we may have to stay with them and wait out the storm.

It is always a challenge to respond rationally when children act up. It is especially difficult when they're headed for a tantrum in public. But with practice, we can become as effective and skillful as Juan's mother. She was waiting for a prescription at the pharmacy when Juan, five, removed a toy from a display rack:

Juan: I want this, Mommy.
Mom: Not now, Juan. I just came in to pick up my prescription.
Juan: But I really want it. It's exactly what I wanted for a long, long time.
Mom: I know, but not today. Your birthday is coming, though.
Juan: I want my present NOW!
Mom: I know how much you want it, Juan. But I can't buy it for you now.
Juan: I'm going to hit you if you don't get it for me.

He took a swing at her.

Mom: (*firmly*) You may not hit me. I am leaving now. The toy must be put back.

She hastily paid for her prescription and headed toward the door. Juan followed, still clutching the toy.

Juan: I'm taking it.
Mom: The toy is not paid for; it needs to be put back.
Juan: NO!
Mom: Taking something without paying for it is stealing. Stealing is against the law.
Juan: You put it back.
Mom: I didn't take it. I'll wait right here for you while you return it.

Juan reluctantly put the toy on the display rack. When he came back, his mother said, "It must have been very hard to give up something you wanted so much."

When I read this dialogue to parents, they are amazed and envious of Juan's mother's skills. She is a model for us all but, as she admits, "I can only do this on a good day."

Had she been less skillful, she might have snatched the toy away and dragged him out of the store with an angry lecture or threat of punishment. Instead, she stated firmly what needed to be done ("The toy must be put back"). She set limits clearly ("I can't buy it for you now. . . . You may not hit me. . . . The toy is not paid for; it needs to be put back"). She taught values without accusing him ("Taking something without paying for it is stealing. Stealing is against the law"). Young children take seriously statements like "It's against the law" or "The rule is . . ."

When Juan finally returned the toy, his mother showed great empathy by saying, "It must have been very hard to give up something you wanted so much." By ending with that remark, she turned a potential battle into an opportunity for Juan to feel good about himself because of what he had been able to do. Juan learned limits without being punished. By combining a variety of skills (describing the problem, acknowledging his feelings and teaching limits without attacking him), Juan's mother rendered punishment unnecessary and turned the situation into a powerful learning experience.

Some parents believe that love and good intentions are all we need to discipline our children. I believe that love isn't enough. We need more. Like Juan's mother, we need skills that help us find alternatives to punishment.

5

"They Make Me So Mad!"

Dealing with Our Anger

"I never knew I had a temper until I had children. No one told me I could get so enraged at someone I love so much."

"When he hits his little sister, I want to smack him to let him know what it feels like."

"Sure, I love her. But I don't always like her."

"My daughter was sick and refused to take her medicine. I became almost crazy. I had to leave the room because I was afraid I was going to force it down her throat. It became such a struggle of wills— this tiny person made me feel totally inadequate."

"When he wouldn't get dressed on time and kept dawdling and the clock kept ticking, I wanted to kill him."

"When she starts whining, I want to shake her till she shuts up."

"My mother was a yeller and a hitter and I resolved I'd never do that with my own children. But it is the first thing I do when they defy me."

To people who do not have children, these words may sound like a chorus of potential child abusers, but they are the words of loving, responsible parents. Until they have children, most adults never imagine the fury a child can inspire. And what makes our rage so frightening is that it is directed at the very people we care most about.

We rarely talk about how enraged children can make us. We may feel guilty because a child can send us into a temper tantrum as unharnessed as his own. We deeply regret the vengeful, abusive words we cannot take back. We feel that there is something wrong with us because we explode. But normal parents become enraged by normal children. Intense anger toward children is inevitable no matter how much we love them.

In the heat of a confrontation we often *want* to hurt our children, get back at them, humiliate them, punish them because they have made us feel so powerless. We need to try to resist that urge for revenge because our long-term goal is to change behavior, not to inflict pain. And after we do cause emotional or physical pain, instead of feeling relieved, most parents feel worse.

A Better Way

"I start out calm but as their demands go on and on, I feel myself going out of control. I get excited and angry. While it's happening, I know there has to be a better way but I don't know what the better way is."

When children elicit our rage, what can we do to limit the damage our anger may cause them as well as us? You cannot pretend to be calm and rational when you are not. You need to express anger, but *how* you express it is crucial if you want to avoid hurting your child.

What are our alternatives to hitting or hurling insults?

1. Use words that express *your* feelings instead of attacking the child. Make a *brief*, strong statement: "I am very angry about . . ." Depending on the circumstances, you may want to add a short statement about your expectations: "I expect this new coat to be hung up, not dumped on the floor." Say nothing about the child's character or personality ("You're such a slob"). We can say how we feel, not how "rotten" they are.

2. *Exit*—the best four-letter word for an angry confrontation. Removing yourself from the scene gives you time to cool down and think about what you'll say when you see the child again.

3. Make amends when the storm has blown over. You can restore loving feelings and let your children know that your anger—no matter how intense—is not permanent.

Brief Expressions of Anger

Dad: Tina, get your ass up here now! Look at this pigsty. You're getting messier every day. Why can't you ever hang up your clothes? I refuse to buy you any more clothes if you're just going to throw them all around.

Tina: Why don't you ever yell at Tommy? His room is messy, too. You're mean.

Dad threw up his hands, slammed the door and, as he stomped downstairs, yelled loudly about never buying Tina any more clothes. His anger was understandable—Tina's room was a mess. He was frustrated with her continuous failure to keep a tidy room but his anger was not constructive; it did not encourage her to change. He attacked Tina ("You're getting messier every day"). He barked an insulting order ("Get your ass up here") and he threatened ("I refuse to buy you any more clothes if . . ."). His attack, order and threat only brought on Tina's defiance, making her as angry as he was. She never even heard the message he intended to give, which was to clean her room.

Had Tina's father chosen other words to express his exasperation, such as "I really get mad when I see those clothes tossed all over your room . . .", there is no guarantee that she would have scurried to scour her room, but Tina would not have counterattacked with "Why don't you ever yell at Tommy?" He might have given her a chance to work out a plan to keep her room neater, which would have avoided a confrontation that left them both angry.

Our aim is to use the enormous energy of our anger less destructively. We need to begin our statements with "I" or "My" ("My blood boils when . . .") rather than "You." An angry statement beginning with "You" will inevitably become a personal attack on the child's character. She will react with hurt, defiance or resentment, and the attack will have accomplished nothing toward solving the problem.

Statements of anger are most effective when they are *brief*. A brief statement makes us more authoritative. The longer we talk, the more our children tune us out. Most children will listen to one firm sentence about our feelings ("I really get incensed when I call you to dinner three times and I'm totally ignored") because they *do* care about how we feel.

John, three, and his mother were shopping when he began begging for several kinds of sugar-coated cereals, which she refused to buy. As his pleas grew more adamant, she found herself becoming angrier.

John: *(loudly)* If you won't buy these, you're a stupid jerk.
Mom: I get very angry when I'm called names.
John: I don't care. You're a dirty dumbhead.

Mom: I won't be called names. I don't even feel like listening when I'm talked to that way.

John: Well, I don't want to talk to you ever again.

Mom: I see how angry you are. Maybe you'll feel like talking to me later.

She walked toward the checkout counter and John followed. Later in the car, John said, "Mommy, I'm sorry I called you names. Are you still mad at me?"

John's mother had been furious at being called dumb and stupid but she responded with a brief statement of her feelings ("I get very angry when I'm called names") instead of counterattacking. When he called her a "dirty dumbhead," she was tempted to counter with "You have such a fresh mouth. Don't you dare talk to me like that again!" But she stayed on the track of expressing her feelings briefly and she even added another skill: she acknowledged his feelings by saying, "I see how angry you are," and she showed him that name-calling wouldn't get him what he wanted.

Their struggle was resolved because she expressed her anger without damaging John. His apology would never have come about if she hadn't briefly stated her anger and acknowledged his feelings. His question, "Are you still mad at me?" shows how much children need our good feelings.

Four-year-old Kyle frequently hit and kicked. His mother tried to help him translate his frustration into words. When he struck out, she held his wrists and said firmly, "No hitting. Tell me how you feel in words." Little by little, he began to substitute words for fists. His mother thought they were making progress until one afternoon when he didn't want to leave the playground. His unanticipated tantrum pushed her into a rage of her own:

Kyle: *(whining)* I don't want to go home. I want to stay here.

Mom: We have to go now.

Kyle began to kick her.

Mom: No kicking. Tell me in words.
Kyle: *(loudly)* Mommy is a baby. You're caca. You're a pee-pee doody. I hate you.

She exploded, dragged him home and washed his mouth out with soap. Her fury was understandable; she was acutely embarrassed. But her way of striking back was invasive and humiliating. Even more importantly, Kyle learned he could not trust his mother. She had told him to express his feelings in words and when he did, she punished him. The message he received was, "I can't believe my mother."

In the heat of daily confrontations, children often lash back with "I hate you" or "You don't love me." When we are genuinely angry with them, we *don't* feel loving. If they say, "You don't love me," we often answer, "Oh, yes, I do." But they still hear the anger in our voice. That is confusing to children. When our words and our tone of voice are contradictory, they get mixed messages and cannot trust their perception. They do not know whether to believe their instincts or our words.

A more authentic response to "You don't love me" would be, "Right now I'm feeling very cross and I don't feel like talking about love. I feel like talking about the toys that aren't put away . . . the spill that must be mopped up . . . the hitting that needs to stop . . . the dog that has to be taken out . . ." Later, when your anger has subsided, you can reassure your child that your loving feelings have returned.

Exit—The Four-Letter Word That Works

Mom: Linda, would you please feed the cats now?

Linda: I'm not your maid.
Mom: *(raging inside)* I won't even discuss that statement.

She left the kitchen. When she had cooled off, she returned.

Mom: If you want to do a job other than feeding the cats, we can talk about it.
Linda: What job?
Mom: I'll have to think about it.
Linda: I think I will feed the cats. It makes them like me more.

Sometimes we get frustrated because we have to go through the same routine over and over. "Will Linda ever feed the cats without my reminding her?" When our wrath builds, exiting from the scene can put a physical stop to our outbursts before they become damaging. Exiting gives us a chance to express our anger in ways that we will not regret later. Some parents go into the bathroom and cry or take a shower. Others turn up the radio and swear. Some pound pillows and others write angry notes. For Linda's mother, walking out of the kitchen bought her some time to cool off and to think of how she might offer Linda a choice that would pull them both out of this confrontation.

Five minutes before leaving for nursery school, Neil put on his superhero cape. As both Neil and his mother knew, Neil's teacher did not allow capes or other costumes in the classroom.

Mom: You know you can't wear that cape till after school.
Neil: No, IN school.
Mom: *(impatiently)* Remember, your teacher said no superheroes in school.
Neil: Then I won't go to school.
Mom: *(now furious)* Okay, then don't!

Neil: *(brightly)* We'll do something else.

Mom: *(exploding)* If you don't go, you'll have to stay in your room all day. No TV. No going outside.

Mom left the kitchen for five minutes. When she was calmer, she returned:

Mom: Let's erase what just happened. You really want to pretend you're a superhero, right?

Neil: Yes.

Mom: I bet it makes you feel strong and powerful when you play superhero.

Neil: Yes.

Mom: Are you ready to get your jacket on now?

Neil: Okay.

Neil put on his jacket, carried the cape to school and stashed it in his cubby.

Neil's mother exited from the superhero scene because she knew her anger was growing to a point where she was about to say or do something damaging to Neil. During her brief time away from him, she realized that she did not have to "control" him. Those few minutes alone let her see more clearly that the cape was in the teacher's domain, so she decided to let the teacher deal with it.

Time alone for a few moments allows us to become more rational, to think about a better solution and to rehearse what we want to say when we rejoin the child.

What does make us so angry with children? Usually it is a feeling of helplessness which stems from our inability to be in control. Many parents have the illusion that they are *supposed* to control children.

If a child behaves in ways that seem negative or unacceptable, the mother is told that she should not "let" him

behave that way, that she should "make" him behave. . . . If she can't control the "bad" behavior of her
child, she feels like a bad mother, an inadequate mother,
an incompetent mother. His behavior threatens her self-
image and . . . her inability to make him do what she
wants provokes greater anger and makes her feel out of
control herself.*

When children misbehave we believe that it reflects badly
on us. When we cannot control them, we are resentful that
they embarrass us, defy us, ignore us, disappoint us.

Exiting is not possible if we are in public, or if leaving the
child alone would present any danger. But if we do feel we
are about to explode in public and become embarrassed as
an audience of strangers stares at us and at our children, we
can say to ourselves, "Thank goodness these people are
strangers and I'll never see them again." It is more important
to focus on the child's immediate need and our own than to
appear as the "good parent."

Every Sunday morning Suzi's father enjoyed cooking a big
breakfast for the family:

Suzi: I hate eggs. Why do we always have to have eggs?
Dad: Just eat your eggs, Suzi. You know you haven't had
them in a week. We're out of cold cereal and you
don't like hot cereal.

Suzi picked at her eggs with disgust. Dad furiously grabbed
her plate and took it away.

Dad: Okay, go hungry. It's the last time I'll make breakfast
for you.
Suzi: I don't care.

*Elaine Heffner, *Mothering* (New York: Doubleday, 1978), p. 59.

Dad: When I cook for you, all you do is give me aggra-
       vation.

Suzi's father took her rejection personally and became furious because he could not *make* her enjoy the eggs. He thought
to himself, "I went to the trouble of cooking for you, so eat
and stop giving me a hard time." He issued a command: "Just
eat your eggs." He offered an irrelevant explanation to induce
her to eat the eggs: "We're out of cold cereal . . . You don't
like hot cereal" implied that something was wrong with Suzi,
as if all virtuous children liked hot cereal. His words, "Okay,
go hungry," were rejecting and punitive. To maintain her
pride, she retorted, "I don't care." Suzi's father could have
benefited from an exit and avoided their final deadlock.

When children irritate us, we often attribute their motives
to "trying to get us," "being manipulative" or "doing it on
purpose," and our anger intensifies because we take it personally. Jason's mother described how her two-year-old "purposely" dropped his fork on the floor repeatedly "just to get
me mad." She said to herself, "Why is he doing this to me?"
That question made it impossible for her to state calmly,
"Jason, the fork is for eating, not for dropping." Her anger
was exacerbated because she saw his behavior as purposely
designed to annoy her, rather than realizing that, to a toddler,
dropping things repeatedly is a fascinating, irresistible game.

Restoring Loving Feelings

Rage sometimes gets the better of us. No matter how good
our intentions, there will be times when we are unable to
restrain ourselves in time to make a brief statement of our
anger or to exit. But it is reassuring to know that even after
an angry outburst, you can still establish rapport with your
child once again. Sometimes an apology is appropriate, or

you can make amends with humor. After the air has cleared you can examine the problem that has caused your rage and find more helpful solutions.

At the end of a stressful day at work, Curt's mother had just served herself spaghetti when Curt, four, hopped up from his chair and knocked her plate off the table. Spaghetti and sauce splattered all over the floor.

Mom: Son of a bitch!

Curt: Mommy, everyone makes mistakes. Remember when you dropped the bottle of orange juice?

Mom: *(picking up shards of plate and hurling them into the trash can)* "Yes, but I can't even eat my goddamn food in peace. I am sick of your jumping up and down, up and down during my meal. You will sit at the table and finish eating until you are excused. IS THAT CLEAR?

Curt sat silently and waited for the storm to blow over. Mother's dinner was ruined. An hour later, she approached Curt:

Mom: I really had a temper tantrum when that plate broke. I was so angry with myself for screaming at you when I know you didn't do it on purpose.

Curt: But why did you yell at ME?

Mom: Because you were the closest one to me. Who else could I yell at?

Curt laughed.

An accidental spill at a moment when she was tired and hungry was enough to ignite Curt's mother's fuse. But afterward she was able to make amends by using a term, "temper tantrum," that Curt could easily identify with. She lightened the mood by injecting humor ("Because you were the closest one to me") and restored good feelings without

wallowing in guilt. She did not say, for example, "I'm a terrible mother for saying those things to you." Curt needed to know (as do all children) that when parents get angry and lose control, their loving relationships are not permanently severed.

When we make amends, children are usually forgiving because our good feelings are so essential to them. They can also be highly perceptive, as Krista, five, was when talking quietly with her father after an angry scene:

Krista: Daddy, when you shout, I can't hear you.
Dad: You can't *hear* me when I shout?
Krista: No. When you are angry at me and shout, I get mad at you.
Dad: Sometimes when I'm angry, I guess I do shout.
Krista: But you don't have to shout. You could just tell me you're angry and talk.
Dad: That sounds like a good idea. Will you listen then?
Krista: Maybe. But if you shout at me, I'll get angry and shout back at you, and I won't be your friend.

Two exchanges illustrate the difference between a parent who is unforgiving and another who can restore loving feelings after a sudden outburst:

Mom: Mandy, you must take your bath now.
Mandy: Well, I don't want to.
Mom: Okay, either you take your bath or go straight to bed.

Mandy stood without moving, arms crossed, defiantly.

Mom: (*yelling*) All right. Get to bed this minute!

Mandy ran to her room crying and her mother slammed the door. Two minutes later, Mandy emerged, wearing a bathrobe.

Mandy: Mommy, I do want to take a bath.
Mom: Too bad. Too late. Tough nuggies. Go to bed dirty.

When Mandy began to defy her, Mother became furious. Uncomfortable with her mother's anger, Mandy did try to make amends but her mother didn't let her. Every child needs a second chance and an opportunity to be forgiven.

A parent who can make amends after a bitter confrontation restores the loving bond with her child. Inevitably we will say things when enraged that we will later wish we'd never said. But when the storm has abated, we can say, "I wish I hadn't talked that way to you."

Three-and-a-half-year-old Philip had a history of biting other children, but he had not done so for many months. He and his mother were at the playground when Philip noticed one of his previous victims and approached her. The little girl's mother saw Philip and moved protectively toward her daughter. Suddenly the little girl cried and her mother shrieked, "He bit her! He bit her!"

Mom: *(furious and humiliated)* Philip, come here this min-
        ute!
Philip: I only kissed her.
Mom: I don't believe it! You're lying.

She dragged Philip away while the little girl screamed. Philip's mother felt her rage grow to fury. As soon as they arrived home, Philip protested repeatedly, "I didn't bite her. I wanted to kiss her and she wouldn't let me."

Mom: If this is the way you're going to behave, I'm not
        taking you anywhere again.
Philip: I didn't do anything to her.

Totally beside herself, she grabbed his shoulders and shook him. Then she slapped him in the face.

Mom: Philip, I thought you'd stopped biting. I can't take
        you anywhere. I don't believe what you just did.
        Are you an animal or a little boy? I am sick about
        this. Go to your room.

She felt half-crazed. She sent him to his room because she feared what she might do to him if they remained together. She lay on the sofa for several minutes. Her temper slowly subsided and she was sick with remorse. When she felt more composed, she knocked on Philip's door. He was stretched across his bed with his shoes still on. Mother sat on the bed beside him and he took her hand silently. She removed his shoes and emptied their contents—several tablespoonsful of playground sand—into the wastebasket.

Mom: I wish I didn't get so mad and hit you.
Philip: I just wanted to kiss her and she didn't want to. *(He began to cry.)* I'm sorry, Mommy. I didn't mean to bite her.

With tears streaming down both their cheeks, she hugged him.

Mom: Oh, Philip, what can I do to help you?
Philip: I wanted to be friends only. But nobody at the playground was nice to me. That big boy called me names and pushed me.
Mom: It's hard to make friends with new people, but you can't do it by hurting them.
Philip: I know. But why did she scream? I only wanted to kiss her.
Mom: Maybe when you feel like kissing a stranger, you could tell me and give me a kiss instead. What do you think?
Philip: Okay, Mommy. I love you.

At a museum a few days later, Philip saw another little girl and started talking to her. He then ran to his mother and whispered, "I feel like I want to give you a kiss, Mommy."

Mom: Philip, you remembered!

When I read this dialogue in a workshop, parents breathe an immense sigh of relief because they can identify with Philip's mother. It gives them a chance to talk about their own intense anger with their children. Anger is one of the most painful issues we struggle with because our children can enrage us more than anyone else in ways we never thought possible before we became parents. But with practice and effort we can learn to express our anger less destructively.

6

Constructive
Criticism Isn't
Building Self-Esteem

Mom: How many times do I have to tell you not to lose
your things? You're always so irresponsible. Yesterday you forgot your lunch. Wednesday you left
your glasses at school. Tuesday you lost your bus
pass and Monday you lost your math homework.
You're *always* losing things. What am I going to do
with you?

Allen: *(dejectedly)* Well, I guess I'm just a loser.

With all the best intentions, many parents think that they
can make a child change for the better by pointing out what
is wrong with him. But the sad fact is, criticism reinforces
the very behavior we're trying to correct.

Children take criticism from a parent very personally. They
feel attacked by someone whose admiration they crave.
Sometimes criticism convinces them that they cannot change
and, like nine-year-old Allen, they see themselves as losers.
In other cases, critical attacks make children defensive so
they retaliate with hostility and defiance. Either way, criticism gives children no incentive to change.

Many parents who are new to my workshops ask, "But
how can I teach my children without criticizing their be-

havior, manners and bad habits?" There are numerous ways, but first let's look more closely at the nature of criticism and what it does to a child.

Criticism is justified as a teaching method when it is called "constructive criticism." But can criticism really be constructive? To criticize means to judge, evaluate, blame, censure or condemn. To construct means to build. Can you build a child up by tearing him down? Can you build responsibility, competence, motivation in your children by judging, blaming, condemning? No. Even when we feel we are being "constructive" by pointing out a child's shortcomings, criticism will have one or more of these effects:

—It will make him see himself as a loser.

—It will make him defensive or defiant.

—It will rob him of any motivation or desire to try something new.

As a child, Nathaniel's father had to work in the family store after school and never had a chance to play sports. As an adult, he took up tennis with a passion. He also became heavily involved in Nathaniel's performance. Watching his son play, he commented on every shot:

"Why don't you watch the ball?"

"What's the matter with you? You were daydreaming!"

"You missed three easy lobs in a row."

"Just keep your eye on the ball."

"Concentrate—lean into the shot—hit it sooner . . ."

His father seemed to take each of Nathaniel's shots as a personal triumph or affront. He thought he was offering his son constructive criticism that would improve the boy's tennis game. Nathaniel might have been able to accept such words from a coach whose job was to instruct, but when he heard them from his father, he said to himself, "I'm not good enough. I can never please Dad. I'll never be a success at this game." And he soon stopped playing tennis entirely.

Like Allen, Nathaniel came to see himself as a loser after what felt like a barrage of criticism.

Criticism can also create anger and defiance. In many families criticism is verbal poison that eats away at parent-child relationships. If you recall how you felt when your parents criticized you, you may understand what your own children hear in your critical statements. At one of my workshops a father recalled his own father's biting words: "My dad was always nitpicking at me for little things: 'straighten your tie . . . comb your hair more neatly . . . tuck in your shirt . . . stop slumping.' His words undermined me so. I needed *not* to listen to him. Even now, at the age of forty, if I were falling off a cliff and he told me to grab a branch, I wouldn't do it."

Mom: Do you want me to listen to you practice your lines for the class play?
Ellie: Yes, please listen.
Mom: Okay, go ahead.

Ellie, ten, recited well at first but stumbled and became more hesitant as she proceeded. Her mother corrected every word.

Mom: Don't run your words together. Slow down and say them clearly. These are very easy lines.
Ellie: I'm trying.

But she continued to make mistakes.

Mom: If you'd been working on your lines all along, and practiced them every day like you're supposed to, you wouldn't be forgetting so many.
Ellie: Don't bug me!
Mom: (*anxiously*) This play is coming up next week. How do you expect to learn your part by then? Emily already knows her part.

Ellie: Get out of my room. I don't want your help.

Instead of helping Ellie memorize her lines, her mother's criticism had the opposite effect. Ellie grew angry. When her mother pointed out what Ellie already knew ("If you'd been working on your lines all along, and practiced them every day like you're supposed to, you wouldn't be forgetting so many"), Ellie quite naturally retorted "Don't bug me!" Her mother also compared Ellie with another child ("Emily already knows her part") which only made Ellie feel more inadequate. And she downplayed the difficulty of memorizing the lines ("These are very easy lines").

When a child is struggling with homework, music lessons or athletic skills, the best way to discourage her is to say, "It's easy." If you want to motivate a child to keep at a task, do just the opposite and say, "It's not easy, is it? But I'll bet you can do it."

Sam's mother also thought she could change her twelve-year-old son's tendency toward sedentary activities by criticizing him:

Mom: I'm going running, Sam. How about joining me?

Sam: I don't feel like it.

Mom: Why not? You're still in your pajamas watching TV.

Sam: Maybe later.

Mom: That's what you always say. It's a gorgeous day and the exercise would be good for you.

Sam: Leave me alone.

Mom: Listen to me! You're going to be a weakling. You never do anything physical. If you had your way, you'd do nothing but eat candy and watch television all day.

Sam: *(choking back tears)* No, I wouldn't!

Criticism is particularly lethal to preadolescents and adolescents because they are already so self-conscious about their appearance and changes in their bodies. When we nag them about their weight, their makeup, the length of their hair, or their grubby jeans, we reinforce their negative feelings about themselves. Younger children, too, absorb our criticism like sponges because they see themselves through our eyes.

Criticism from those we love erodes our self-image and discourages motivation. Many children feel it is safer not to try than to risk failure, so they react to criticism by agreeing with it:

Parent's remark	*Child's interpretation*
"Why can't you figure that out? It's so simple. If you'd just read the problem more carefully, you'd understand it."	"Maybe I really am a dope. I never will learn."
"If only you'd try harder, you'd be able to do better. You give up too easily."	"Why should I try? I'll never get it anyway."

Jane, eight, was excited about an upcoming family gathering and wanted to participate in the preparations.

Jane: I'm drawing place cards for dinner. May I please borrow your pen and ink, Dad?

Dad: Maybe you'd better use a marking pen. Pen and ink can make a mess.

Jane: But I want a fine line.

Dad: You may smear it. You'll ruin the cards.

Jane: No, I won't.

Dad: I'll watch you practice on scrap paper. But be careful.
Jane: Oh, never mind. I guess you're right. I'll use markers.

Jane's father didn't openly criticize her; he didn't say anything as direct as, "You're sloppy." But he certainly implied that she was by saying, "You may smear it. You'll ruin the cards." Before she even began, he took away her desire to try pen and ink when he said, "I'll watch you practice on scrap paper. But be careful." Jane took the safe way out. She gave up, saying, "I guess you're right."

Often we are unaware that we are criticizing a child. We may be replaying the tapes we grew up hearing ("Why don't you watch where you're going? You are such a klutz! . . . Why don't you want to go to the birthday party? Everyone else is going. . . . Why don't you ever sit up straight at the table?"). We may even think we're being helpful, like Nick's father who thought he could help Nick improve his football skills:

Dad: How did you get that bruise on your chin?
Nick: Playing football. It really hurt, too.
Dad: *(sarcastically)* You tackle with your chin? What a way to play football!
Nick: *(angrily)* I tried my hardest, Dad.
Dad: If you tackle right, you can bring down the biggest kid.
Nick: You sound like I did it on purpose, Dad. Thanks a lot.

Nick's father may have meant well but his words, "If you tackle right, you can bring down the biggest kid," only showed eleven-year-old Nick what a disappointment he was to his father. The comment didn't help Nick become a better tackle; it made him feel inept and clumsy. No parent consciously

Drawing by Drucker; © 1985
The New Yorker Magazine, Inc.

"And good night to all my critics!"

sets out to humiliate a child. But without intending to, that is what Nick's father did.

Leah's mother never dreamed she was being critical—and she actually wasn't—but children hear everything in relation to themselves. When her mother realized that Leah, nine, heard her remarks as critical, she recouped:

Mom: Your friend Samantha has such nice manners. I noticed how she always says "please" and "thank you" when she comes over here.

Leah: You mean *I* don't have good manners?

Mom: Your ego is so fragile that I can't even praise your friends?

Leah: Well, isn't that what you meant?

Mom: No. That's not how I feel. In fact, I remember just the other day when you were so polite and kind to Grandma. When she came to visit, you hung up her coat and later found her glasses for her.

Although she hadn't intended to say anything negative about Leah, when she heard her daughter's reaction, Mother skillfully turned the situation around and used it as an occasion to boost Leah's self-esteem.

We are sometimes unaware that when we criticize before the fact, we set the stage for a self-fulfilling prophecy. As Jill's mother was on her way out for the evening, she said, "Jill, I want you to be a good girl and not pick on your little brother while the sitter is here." Jill's mother was expecting misbehavior before it occurred. Perhaps she had reason to, based on Jill's previous behavior. But Jill heard the implicit message: "Mom expects me to pick on him." And she fulfilled the prophecy by teasing and tormenting her brother.

So many parents come to my workshop with the question, "How can I teach my children to behave?" We discuss how hard it is not to criticize a child's faults and we examine how criticism backfires. Then we begin to look at alternatives to criticism, alternatives that improve a child's behavior without attacking his self-esteem. Some of these techniques have been discussed in earlier chapters and will be expanded upon here. Others are new. But all these approaches can help guide a child to behave in ways that make him feel good about himself. And the child who feels right finds it easier to act right.

When things go wrong—and they inevitably do—you can point at the situation instead of pointing at the child. You can talk about what needs to be done rather than how errant the child is. For example:

	Rather than
"Ice cream that's left out on the counter will turn to soup."	"You're always so careless. Don't you know that you thoughtlessly left the ice-cream carton on the counter? Where's your head, in the clouds?"
"The dirty dishes belong in the dishwasher, not on the table."	"How many times do I have to remind you? What do you think this is, a res-taurant?"

If your statement is directed at the deed rather than the doer, your children won't hear it as a personal attack.

Jim's family rarely completed a meal without eight-year-old Jim's overturning a glass or spilling food. His parents were making a concerted effort to stop uttering their usual criticisms ("Can't you be more careful? . . . Why can't we get through a meal without one of your disasters?"). One night when Jim gave a bottle of steak sauce a vigorous shake without noticing that the cap was loose, large dollops of sauce flew across the table and onto his father's shirt. About to explode, his father swallowed hard and said through clenched teeth, "This mess needs a wet sponge." Shocked at this atyp-ical reaction, Jim looked at his father with enormous gratitude and went to get a sponge. After a few moments of awkward silence, Jim said, "You know, Dad, the next time I'm going to check the top first."

If Jim's father had burst out with his usual remarks ("Damn it, Jim! Why the hell didn't you check the top first?"), Jim would have become angry with his father. Jim would never have been able to say, ". . . next time I'm going to check the top . . ." His father's restraint, as difficult as it was, allowed Jim to feel genuinely sorry and to learn from the incident.

In Chapter 4 we talked about substituting consequences for punishment. We also can use consequences as an alternative to criticism. And when we do, the child often comes away from the experience feeling competent and confident.

On a warm May morning, five-year-old Tara wanted to wear the same red wool skirt she'd chosen every day for a week.

Mom: It's very warm today, honey. You'll be too hot if you wear a wool skirt.

Tara: No, I won't. I want my red skirt.

Mom: It's ridiculous to wear a winter skirt on a warm day. Wear your cotton overalls today.

Tara: No, I want my red skirt *only*.

Tara began to cry and disappeared into her closet in search of the favorite skirt.

Mom: *(dragging her out of the closet)* Enough talk. Get dressed this minute.

Tara: Only if I can wear my red skirt.

Mom: *(furious with this recurring ritual)* NOW I'm really mad. Put on these overalls or I'll leave without you.

Tara: NO, I won't! And I'm not going to school.

Tara's mother put Tara in a defensive position. The statement "It's ridiculous to wear a winter skirt on a warm day" challenged her to defy her mother. Tara focused all her emotional energy on getting back at her mother: "NO, I won't! And I'm not going to school." But a few days later, Tara's mother tried another approach. She decided to let consequences take over the teaching role:

Mom: What are you going to wear today?

Tara: My red wool skirt.

Mom: Okay, it's your choice.

Tara: *(surprised)* Is it cold today?

Mom: No. The weatherman said it will be very warm.

Tara: And it's okay to wear my heavy wool winter skirt?

Mom: If you want to.

Tara: Good.

Tara finished dressing and climbed onto a chair to see herself in the mirror.

Tara: I really look good today, don't I?

Mom: Yes, you do.

Her mother decided that it was more important that Tara feel good about herself. If Tara was uncomfortable on a warm day, that would be a harmless consequence and maybe she would decide on her own that wearing the red skirt wasn't a good idea.

Another way to avoid criticism is to invite the child to become a problem solver. After a sports injury, Ted was told by the doctor to exercise his knees regularly. But he was a busy and forgetful eleven-year-old and he let the exercises lapse:

Dad: Did you do your knee exercises last night?

Ted: Well, I did the stretching part.

Dad: Good for you! You sure have a lot of things to re-member in your life, don't you?

Ted: I sure do.

Dad: What can we do to help you remember the rest of the exercises?

Ted: You could keep reminding me.

Dad: I don't like that idea. It's not my knees that need strengthening. Anyway, my reminding you always turns into nagging.

Ted: That's for sure.
Dad: Let's work out something so that it's easier for you to remember.
Ted: What if I made a list and put it on my bulletin board?
Dad: Is that something you look at every day?
Ted: Yeah. I think that'll work.

Instead of criticizing Ted for doing only part of the exercise program, his father first pointed to the positive ("Good for you! You sure have a lot of things to remember in your life, don't you?"). Then he approached the problem as something to be solved ("What can we do to help you remember . . . ?"). Because he was drawn in as a problem solver, Ted felt motivated ("What if I made a list . . . I think that'll work").

Another way to gain a child's cooperation or change his behavior without nagging and attacking is to write notes; if you can make them humorous, so much the better. A number of parents say that notes sometimes encourage children to write back and help them enjoy writing. Here are some of the notes parents have used:

> *Please pick me up so you can walk across your room without stepping on me.*
>
> *—Your clothes*

> *Help wanted: To clean bathroom, close shampoo bottle, cap toothpaste tube, hang up wet towels. REWARD: A very pleased mother.*

> *Help!!! Please take me out before I overflow.*
>
> *Love,*
> *The Trash*

Still another substitute for criticism is the motivating statement. When children are in a difficult spot, we're often tempted to attack them for getting into that spot: "If only you'd listened to me first. . . . What's the matter with you?" But it is far more helpful if we make a statement that helps them believe they can tackle the problem, such as "That's not an easy assignment, is it?" . . . "That's a dilemma. What do you think you could do about it?" . . . "I know that's a hard job and I see you are really making an effort."

Evan's father started out on the criticism track but found a way to help his ten-year-old son when he was discouraged about his chess game. Dad had given Evan an advantage by doing without a queen but Evan lost anyway:

Dad: Evan, what *are* we going to do about your chess game?
Evan: Thanks a lot, Dad! You really make me feel lousy.
Dad: Well, you were so far ahead and then you blew it. If you'd just concentrate, you could do it.
Evan: You expect me to be perfect.

At this point, his father recognized Evan's pain and backtracked to acknowledge his son's feelings:

Dad: I really hurt your feelings, didn't I?
Evan: Yes, you did.
Dad: It's bad enough losing without someone making a stupid comment, isn't it?
Evan: Yes, it is. It makes me feel like I don't even want to play anymore.
Dad: Well, I can understand that. Chess is a difficult game. It takes years to learn how to play really well.
Evan: Sometimes I just don't know where to move.
Dad: It's pretty frustrating, isn't it?
Evan: It is! Sometimes I wish you would help me a little.

Dad:	It seems like the last few times we've played, you didn't want me to give advice.
Evan:	Yeah, that's right. I remember.
Dad:	So?
Evan:	Maybe if you would just help me when I ask for help.
Dad:	Do you think that would work?
Evan:	Yes, I think so.
Dad:	Okay. Want to play another game?
Evan:	Okay, sure.

Evan's father made some highly motivating statements: "Chess is a difficult game. It takes years to learn how to play really well. . . . It's pretty frustrating, isn't it?" When Dad blamed the game instead of Evan, Evan no longer felt attacked and was able to tell Dad what was bothering him: "Sometimes I just don't know where to move." Evan was able to come up with a solution of his own about how much help he wanted from his father and when he wanted it. And he was motivated to play another game.

When a child does the same annoying thing over and over, it is extremely difficult to refrain from criticizing ("Why do you *always* do that? . . . Why can't you *ever* . . ."). If your child has a recurring behavior or habit that annoys you, you can anticipate when it will occur. Jamie's parents found that criticism never helped break their son's irritating habit of asking to make a bathroom stop only minutes after beginning each car trip. Their usual responses were "Why didn't you go before we left home? You always ask us to stop as soon as we start out!" When his parents recognized this fruitless pattern, they decided to try two new alternatives: Before leaving the house they made a light, impersonal comment such as "Let's all make a bathroom visit before we hit the road," instead of the old routine, "You'd better go now,

Jamie, so you don't ask us to stop in five minutes like you always do." Then, when Jamie did ask for a stop once they were in the car, Dad said, "I know you really have to go, Jamie. I'll pull over the first chance I get. Can you wait that long?"

Jamie's father told our workshop that the first time he tried this new response Jamie was surprised and appreciative. Their car trips became more enjoyable and Jamie's requests grew less frequent.

Another way to avoid damaging effects of criticism is to withhold the critical remark that is on the tip of your tongue. Saying nothing may seem nearly impossible at times, but if you can manage to swallow your words, the result may be a pleasant surprise, as Debbie's mother found:

"My daughter's handwriting is bad, her spelling is horrible and she has a lot of difficulty writing stories for school," her mother told a workshop group. "She knows she has a problem in this area and when she had to write an assignment the other night, she asked me to look it over.

"It was terrible—the sloppiest thing I'd ever seen. Spelling errors all over the place, but the subject matter was pretty good. In the past I would have told her that she couldn't turn in such a mess and I would have said, 'Copy it over.'

"But now I've recognized what my criticism does—she gets very upset and says, 'I can't do anything right. You're never satisfied with what I do.' And we get into a big fight. So this time I said nothing about the spelling errors and sloppiness of her handwriting. I simply commented on the good subject matter. And, would you believe it, hers was one of five compositions chosen to be read at the school assembly!"

Several weeks later Debbie's mother reported that Debbie brought her another writing assignment:

Debbie: Want to read my story, Mom?

Mom: *(so she wouldn't see the errors)* Why don't you read it to me?

Debbie read it with great pride.

Mom: You really worked hard on this story. You must be pleased with yourself.

Debbie: Yeah. Can we copy this and save it?

After relaying this dialogue to the workshop group, Debbie's mother commented, "And this was the same kid who didn't want to write anything a month ago!"

Debbie's mother used a lot of skill in withholding criticism of her daughter's spelling and handwriting. She realized that the teacher would help Debbie with those problems. Debbie received a much finer gift from her mother than a lesson in spelling or handwriting. Her mother reinforced Debbie's pride in her work by pointing out only what was positive in the essay.

So often we notice "the red marks" on the history paper, the misspelled word, the incorrect answer to the multiplication problem, the improper punctuation. We carry this habit of noticing what's "wrong" instead of what's "right" about our children beyond schoolwork into other areas of their lives. When you can break that pattern, as Debbie's mother did, and point out the positives, your children tend to become more cooperative, more motivated and more confident.

Praise and Appreciation: The Best Teaching Techniques

Once you have curtailed criticism and substituted alternatives such as letting your child suffer the minor consequences of undesirable behavior, or describing what needs to be done, or letting your child do his own problem solving, or writing humorous notes and making motivating statements, don't stop there. You can add two of the most important skills: praise and appreciation. These are not difficult skills to acquire and practice and they are far more effective than criticism at inspiring good behavior. They are valuable in and of themselves because they build a child's self-esteem.

Jack's mother frequently complained about her son's habit of borrowing her records without returning them or returning them scratched and without jackets. Her repeated criticisms never changed his habit. But on one of the rare occasions when he did return her record in good shape, she made a point of praising him in a concrete, descriptive way:

"I noticed that you carefully put the record back in the cover so it wouldn't get scratched. I can see you're beginning to understand my hang-up about scratched records. I really appreciate it when you respect my things."

When a child does remember to hang up clothes, close the screen door or do a chore without having to be reminded, we need to comment so they know that we noticed. By expressing appreciation of a job well done, you encourage children to do it again. Jack's mother found this to be true when her praise motivated Jack to take greater care of her records.

If we look for every opportunity to praise children for behavior we appreciate, we reinforce their desire to please us and feel good about themselves. A mother whose children frequently fought in the car made sure to comment when they gave her a few rare minutes of tranquillity on their way to get groceries: "I really enjoyed that drive to the store with you; you both got along so well." She found that her children squabbled less often in the car when she noted their peaceful trips.

Brad's lightning method of brushing his teeth in two strokes aggravated his father. To motivate five-year-old Brad to brush more thoroughly, he brought home a superhero toothbrush. As Brad tried it out, Dad said, "I notice that you're brushing very carefully, even the back teeth that are so hard to reach. I bet the dentist will be impressed."

A mother who had had the same problem put on sunglasses when her three-year-old began to brush his teeth. "Wow! They are so bright, I need my dark glasses!" He loved her humorous way of showing her appreciation and asked her each evening, "Mommy, do you need your sunglasses? Are my teeth bright enough?"

Dana's mother was concerned about her four-year-old's clinginess. Dana was afraid to venture out of the house with anyone except her mother or father. Her mother found that the more she criticized Dana for being "silly" or "acting like a baby," the more Dana clung to her skirts. But when Dana went on an outing with an uncle for the first time, her mother used the occasion to foster Dana's courage by praising her:

Mom: You and Uncle Rob went to the toy store together. Just the two of you. That was a pretty grown-up thing to do. You must feel good about that.

Dana: Uncle Rob had fun, too.

When we express our appreciation, we encourage children to repeat appropriate behavior because they genuinely want to please us. And they will only know what pleases us if we tell them.

When eleven-year-old Jeremy returned from trick or treating at exactly 8:00 P.M., his mother said, "I noticed how punctual you were. I really appreciate it when you come home just when I asked you to!" She gave him a hug and he beamed. Her comments were much more effective in helping

Jeremy be on time again than if she had said nothing about his punctuality. Too often we take it for granted when children do what we ask. We might say to ourselves, "Well, I told him to be home by eight. He should be here on time, so why should I mention it?" But it is worth mentioning because children need our appreciation, not our indifference or criticism. If we fail to notice what they do right, they have much less incentive to repeat their good deed.

It is easy to express appreciation or to praise children when they do something noteworthy, something they may have been lax about in the past. It is much more difficult to praise or express appreciation when something goes wrong. But with practice, you can transform some of the most trying situations from negative to positive by using praise and appreciation. The following dialogue may seem extraordinary. You may say, "Oh, I would never be able to do that!" But Tim's mother was able to because she had acquired and practiced these skills over time:

Tim: *(looking ashen)* Mom, something terrible has happened.

Mom: What happened?

Tim: I'm too afraid to tell.

Mom: Are you afraid of my reaction?

Tim: Yes! You're going to kill me.

Mom: Tim, the only way we're going to solve this problem is by talking about it.

Tim: The problem can't be solved.

Mom: As long as you're in one piece, that's all that matters.

Tim: Okay. Here it comes: I broke a plate from your good set, the expensive one.

Mom: I really love those plates, but we can try to replace it.

Tim: Mom, are you sure you aren't very mad?

Mom: Timmy, I am upset, but to me a broken plate is only a broken plate. The important thing is that you came and told me what happened. I appreciate that.

Tim: I wish I hadn't broken it.

Tim's mother skillfully avoided criticizing and blaming, which would only have chipped away at Tim's self-esteem instead of enhancing it. She praised Tim's forthrightness; she reacted with calm when he expected fury; she distinguished between what was important and what was not (". . . a broken plate is only a broken plate"). She wasn't indifferent to the loss of an expensive plate, but she saw it as less significant than Tim's feelings about himself. And most importantly, she showed Tim her appreciation for telling her what happened.

For many of us, responding as Tim's mother did would be extremely difficult. We might hit the ceiling if our child broke an expensive possession. But how would we react if a dinner guest or someone else's child dropped the same plate? We would probably say graciously, "Oh, don't worry. It can easily be replaced." It is ironic that we often find it easier to take care of the feelings of people we care *less* about than those of our children who matter so much more.

Some kinds of praise help children feel good about themselves. Other kinds can backfire.

Jeffrey, five, ran out of school and presented his mother with a broad smile and a basket he'd made for Mother's Day.

"Mommy, Mommy, look what I made for you."

"That's great. You're such a good boy," she said with a quick glance at the basket. Jeffrey's smile collapsed. He looked crushed at her response to the gift he had lovingly produced. Why? She had praised him, hadn't she?

We often think we can build children's self-esteem by lavishing them with praise. We expect them to brim with self-confidence when we tell them how wonderful they are. But when our words are as vague as Jeffrey's mother's words, ("great . . . good"), children may not believe them or us. ("Does she really like my basket? She always says I'm a good boy, but she hardly even looked at my basket.") Jeffrey's mother might have said, "That's such an intricate basket. I see how you wove all those strips of material together. Now the whole family can use it for bread." If she had detailed her observations in this way, Jeffrey might have thought, "She sees how hard I worked on this basket. I guess she really likes it. I've made her happy."

When you praise children, try to describe what they have done as precisely as possible:

> "Instead of waking me this morning, you fixed breakfast all by yourself and I was able to sleep late. That was a big help. And you poured the juice and milk without spilling one single drop!"

> "I see you spelled 'reindeer' correctly on your spelling test. That's a difficult word. I can never remember if the *e* or the *i* follows the *r*."

> "You memorized all those Spanish verbs in just fifteen minutes. That's not easy when they're all so irregular."

When you are precise and descriptive in your praise, children know you have really noticed their accomplishments. But if your words of praise are too general, children may doubt your sincerity.

Sometimes you can't entirely avoid broad adjectives—good, super, wonderful, great—in praising a child, but it is more convincing if they are supplemented with specific descriptions of a child's achievements. When young children bring us their paintings, and grade-school children bring us their reports, it's helpful to respond as Alex's father did. Rather than using sweeping generalizations, he was descriptive:

Alex: Daddy, I made a painting for you. Do you like it?
Dad: Wow! I like these bright colors. Look at all the yellow and red leaves on those trees. It looks like autumn. I'm going to take this to my office and hang it there today.
Alex: You're really going to hang it up at work?
Dad: Sure am.

When his father returned home that evening, he told Alex, "I put that painting in my office and everyone who came in looked at those autumn leaves." Alex smiled proudly.

His father didn't need to play art critic and evaluate Alex's artistic ability. His words effectively praised Alex's effort by pointing out the picture's details; he proved to Alex that he had really enjoyed the painting.

We often praise a child with the words, "I'm proud of you." We mean well with those words but they emphasize the "I" more than the "you." If we really want to praise children, we can reverse those pronouns to give children credit for their own achievement. When a child brings home a report card with an A and we say, "I'm so proud of you," the implication is that *we* are somehow responsible for the A. The pride is *ours*. But if she brings home a report card with a D, we are unlikely to take credit for it. We're more likely to say, "What's the matter with *you*?"

If we say, "*You* must feel good about that grade; it took a lot of work. I'll bet you're proud of yourself," we can encourage our child's pride in her *own* achievement.

Kate, twelve, had worked diligently to learn her part for

the school play. After the performance her parents went backstage. Dad said, "You were so convincing in your role. I could hear all your lines way back in the balcony. You must have been so proud of yourself tonight." Kate's father bolstered her self-esteem by placing the emphasis where it belonged—with Kate herself. Later Kate's mother told her husband, "I could see Kate grow taller before our eyes when you said that. She couldn't stop grinning. I wish I could have preserved that scene on film and caught the look she gave you. Your words meant so much to her." Perhaps without knowing it, Kate's mother did the same thing to her husband as he had done to Kate. By saying "Your words meant so much to her," she put the pride where it belonged. Adults, too, benefit from specific appreciation.

You can also reinforce children's good behavior, motivate them to repeat it and bolster their self-esteem by letting them overhear you praise them in front of another adult:

Susannah just happened to be in the kitchen when her mother was talking on the phone with a friend. "You'll never guess what Susannah did for me today. You know how down I've been since Dad died? Well, Susannah really lifted my spirits today by helping me around the house and by picking a bunch of flowers for me. I was so touched."

As they entered the elevator, Mother said to Danny's father, "Did you notice that Danny has learned to push the open button quickly so no one will be squeezed by the doors?"

"Craig really helped me today. Did you see how he cleared the table and sponged it off?" his mother said to a visiting grandfather while Craig was within earshot.

One caveat: Praising children in front of other adults works better with younger children. Preadolescents and teenagers don't like us to talk about them in front of other people; it only increases their self-consciousness.

Occasionally a parent comes to my workshop and says, "Praise my child? But how can I? Everything he does drives me up the wall! I don't think there's a single thing worth praising." When that happens, I sometimes suggest what I call the "one-a-day technique." Each day find one good thing your child does—no matter how minute or insignificant—and praise him for it.

Eileen was deeply disturbed about her son's "obnoxious" behavior and felt as though they were bickering from dawn to dusk. Randy, ten, provoked her so frequently that she found it difficult to say anything good about him. I asked Eileen to try the one-a-day technique, to write down one thing that he did well each day for the next week and then to praise him for it. She was skeptical at first but the next week she gave me her list:

—Randy, you took out your own splinter. That's hard to do.

—When Joe was getting frustrated with his model, you really helped him put it together. He's lucky to have a friend like you.

—Your baby brother must appreciate it when you get down toys that are too high for him to reach. You really understand what he needs.

—Thanks for coming grocery shopping with me today. I can't remember the last time I was able to finish so quickly.

After a week of being praised for such small, undramatic incidents, Randy improved his behavior markedly. Eileen's husband commented, "I wouldn't have believed it if I hadn't seen it. Until now I couldn't think of a single decent thing he's done in a month."

There is an additional benefit to the one-a-day praise technique: when you are looking for behavior to praise, you aren't focusing so much on the negatives. You won't be so quick to criticize and fewer sparks will fly between you and your children.

While praise and appreciation are valuable tools to teach children what we expect—and they certainly enhance a child's feelings about himself—we do have to be careful about two ways in which praise can backfire. Either it may be threatening or it can hold out expectations that a child fears he cannot meet.

If praise is too lavish, it can be threatening. A child may say to himself, "I know I'm not that terrific." If you say to a child, "You are *always* so honest" or "I'm proud that you *never* lie to me," many children will feel threatened because they know they are not and cannot *always* be so honest. ("He should only know how often I haven't told the truth" or "I wonder when he'll catch me in that lie I told about Bobby.") If we praise with words like "you always" or "you never" children may not believe us or they may feel we're putting them on the spot. If someone said to you, "You always dress so smartly," mightn't you say to yourself, "Ha! She should have seen me three hours ago." Children question such blind praise, too.

Or they find it too high an expectation to meet, as thirteen-year-old Tracy did. She never found academics easy. A typical conversation with her father went like this:

Dad: How's school going this semester?
Tracy: I'm doing okay.
Dad: I told you you were smart.
Tracy: Well, I'm not so smart. I have to work darn hard to get halfway decent marks.
Dad: But I told you if you worked hard, you'd pass and you just said you were doing okay.

Tracy: *(becoming agitated)* So what? Now my teachers will expect me to do this all the time. They can drop dead.

Dad: *(sarcastically)* Success is such a burden!

Tracy slammed her book shut and stormed out of the room. Her father thought he had been encouraging Tracy by telling her that she was smart. But Tracy actually felt threatened by the expectations of her teachers. Fearful of disappointing them, Tracy said to herself, "How can I possibly live up to that?"

When Tracy's father realized that the praise was overwhelming to Tracy, he began to acknowledge her statements without passing judgment on her capabilities. By listening to her perceptions of her schoolwork, he bought some time to gain information. He stopped telling Tracy how smart she was, setting up expectations that she feared she couldn't meet. He realized that by telling her she was smart, he was denying her the credit for working hard, as if good grades would just come naturally. By the end of the next semester their conversations were considerably different:

Tracy: I'm doing better in all my classes.

Dad: It sounds like you're pleased.

Tracy: Yeah, I'm passing everything.

Dad: Every one of your subjects!

Tracy: I bet the teachers are going to expect this all the time.

Dad: I guess sometimes doing well can be scary. If you do something well, you're worried people will expect it again.

Tracy: Yeah, Dad, that's true.

When we've learned to substitute appreciation and descriptive praise for criticism, we can use these new alternatives to teach children responsible behavior even in the most trying circumstances. And the bonus is their bolstered self-esteem. When Owen's mother arrived at school to pick him up, she found him in tears:

Mom: What's wrong?
Owen: I lost my retainer.
Mom: Oh, sweetheart.
Owen: I took it out at lunch and put it in the plastic bag. But then I forgot and I must have dropped it in the garbage with all my lunch stuff.
Mom: Did you look in the garbage?
Owen: Yes, the whole class helped me look. But we couldn't find it. Mom, I feel so bad.
Mom: I know you feel bad. When you get a new retainer, we need to talk about ways not to lose it.
Owen: Mom, aren't you mad at me?
Mom: No, I'm not. I am disturbed about having to buy a new retainer. But I'm not angry with you. Losing it was an accident, not something you did on purpose. Accidents can happen to anyone.

Later,

Owen: Why am I always losing things?
Mom: That's not how I see you. It seems to me you're very concerned about your things. I know you went through all that lunch garbage to look for your retainer. That was a responsible thing to do.

By not lecturing Owen or making him feel worse about himself, his mother indirectly encouraged him to be more responsible. A normal response might have been, "I warned you not to lose that retainer. If you hadn't been so careless at lunch . . ." But Owen's mother had gained the skill of turning even this unfortunate situation into a positive one by finding something to praise ("It seems to me you're very concerned about your things. I know you went through all that lunch garbage to look for your retainer. That was a responsible thing to do.") Owen's mother had learned several skills and had woven them together: she acknowledged his distress ("Oh, sweetheart . . . I know you feel bad"); she avoided blame and criticism; and she invited him to be a problem solver ("When you get a new retainer, we need to talk about ways not to lose it").

It is extremely difficult to avoid criticizing children for losing, breaking or forgetting things. But when we are able to act as their allies instead of blaming them, they will be more motivated to avoid such mishaps.

No child ever has too much self-esteem. If you take every possible opportunity to point out what children do well, praise them descriptively for it and express appreciation, your child will become more cooperative, competent and confident.

7

Learning to
Let Go

"I used to feel that everything in my son's life was my responsibility. But now I realize that it is not my job to make all his decisions for him and protect him every step of the way. My responsibility is to help him become a person who can have a good, happy life by developing his own tools for himself. I'm not responsible for his moods or his mistakes. My job is to help him learn to become competent and capable without having to lean on me."

Until Laura recognized her son as a separate person, she was like most of us—often doing for children what they can do for themselves. From the moment the umbilical cord is cut, a child is a separate individual. We readily accept the fact of physical separation but often we forget that a child is not a psychological extension of ourselves, not our possession, not merely a reflection of us. It is natural to influence and protect our children. But unless we relinquish some control, a child cannot become autonomous, a "self-governed" individual capable of functioning on his own. In matters of clothing, food, homework, free time and other daily concerns, we need to loosen the reins. A child must have a voice in determining what goes into his stomach, what he wears, what he does with his free time and what he is answerable for in his class.

As parents we want to be in control of our children. One way to exercise control is to do as much as possible for them. But the more we do for them, the less they do for themselves and the more they depend on us to make decisions for them. We want to make sure they are healthy and strong, so we decide what they will eat. We want them to look attractive, so we select their clothes and tell them what shirt to wear with which pants. We want them to earn A's, so we correct their homework. We want them to become well-rounded, so we push them into ballet, skating, Little League and art classes.

Our reluctance to let go of our children's emerging identities comes from our need to have children do things *our* way, not theirs. If we let them make their own choices, we run the risk of being embarrassed or feeling helpless when they make mistakes. It can be frightening to let a child face the consequences of her own decisions. But in the end she will learn much more from the experience of living with her choices than from our nagging, intervening or rescuing.

Jayne reminded Patrick, ten, all week that he needed to buy a present for his friend whose birthday party was Saturday. She told him on Thursday that she would not continue to remind him, nor would she run to the store for him at the last moment. She stuck to her guns and on Saturday Patrick went to the party without a present. He faced the consequence of his own forgetfulness. It was difficult for Jayne to let Patrick go without a gift; it would have been easier for her to buy it for him. She worried that his friend would be angry with Patrick or that his friend's mother would consider Jayne an indifferent or inattentive parent. But Jayne was able to "let go" because she decided that getting the present was more Patrick's responsibility than hers. She also knew that not having a present might be embarrassing for Patrick but that he could live through it, and might learn something from it.

From the day a toddler issues her first declaration of independence with a loud, emphatic "NO," the parent-child relationship becomes a tug-of-war between holding on and letting go. The sooner we allow our child a greater say in her own life, the smoother and more loving our relationship will be. And more importantly, the more ready we and our children will be for adolescence when the separation process becomes a necessary, inevitable and often painful source of conflict. Early on, parents can begin to let go in small but significant ways. Giving children choices about what they wear is a good place to start.

Ben's mother had bought him a navy blazer and gray slacks for a large family gathering at Thanksgiving. She was looking forward to showing off her five-year-old son. As she helped Ben dress in his new outfit, he spoke:

Ben: I hate the way I look.
Mom: You do?
Ben: Yeah. Everyone is going to stare at me and say I look cute. And Aunt Esther will pinch my cheek.
Mom: Ummmm.
Ben: Can't I wear my regular clothes?

Mom was stumped. She loved the way he looked in his new blazer and slacks, yet she recognized Ben's discomfort. Unsure, she took some time to think about her answer.

Mom: Well, what "regular clothes"?
Ben: My school clothes, like my corduroy pants and plaid shirt.
Mom: *(pausing)* Ben, if it's that important to you, you may wear the clothes you feel comfortable in.

Ben's mother decided that his feelings about himself were more important than her desire to show him off in a new outfit. Had she insisted on getting her way, she would have sent him the message: "My needs are more important than yours." At a price to herself, Ben's mother "let go."

When Lynette, five, was going through her fancy, frilly stage and wanted to wear her favorite party dress and patent leather shoes to a picnic, her mother suggested that they might be too dressy. "But I let her wear them because I realized she wasn't doing anything bad or harmful by her choice," her mother said. "I just wished I could have worn a large button that said, 'I didn't choose it—she did.' "

Bob McGrath of "Sesame Street" once visited one of my workshops in which parents were discussing conflicts they were having with their children over what they wore to school. He told us that when his daughter was five, she loved wearing layers of skirts. He said his wife wrote this note to the kindergarten teacher:

> *Dear Mrs. Jones,*
> *Alison's taste in clothing does not necessarily reflect the taste of the management.*
>
> > *Sincerely,*
> > *Mrs. McGrath*

Many parents believe they always know what is best for their children—and often they do. But we can't make decisions for our children forever; the issue is how to encourage them to become competent at choosing for themselves. Making their own decisions is a necessary step toward autonomy. We sometimes get in their way by pushing them to do something without considering their needs or wishes. Join the team! Try out for the lead in the play! Go to a museum! As we become more active in managing our children's lives, they may become more passive. And sometimes the more we insist, the more they resent our involvement.

Mom: I have great news for you, girls. I just registered you in a wonderful sculpture class at the Y. It's every Saturday morning and the teacher is marvelous.

Kim: I really don't want to take a class. Saturday is the only day I get to sleep late and watch TV.

Mom: You'll be home by eleven-thirty and you can rest and watch your programs then.

Katherine: I don't want to go either. I don't like getting my hands dirty and working so hard with my fingers.

Mom: Clay is not dirt. And it's not such a strain on your fingers.

Katherine: Well, I don't like classes outside of school. I work hard enough all week.

Mom: I only want you to try it. Give it a fair chance. If you don't like it, you can quit.

Kim: *(sarcastically)* Oh, sure.

Mom: I mean it. Just give it a couple of tries.

Kim: I know I'll hate it.

Mom: You never want to try anything new.

By Saturday morning Mother had coerced Kim and Katherine into going to the sculpture class. They took the course but without enthusiasm. What was the problem? By ignoring their wishes and their need to make choices for themselves, she aroused their resistance. Children want to have a say about their lives, and since school attendance is mandatory, they are understandably possessive about their free time.

Kim and Katherine's mother first ignored their desire to be off-duty on Saturday mornings. Then she contradicted them ("Clay is not dirt. And it's not such a strain on your fingers"). Finally she pressed them into attending the classes. Her own eagerness did not motivate them. It inspired more resistance. ("I know I'll hate it.") Perhaps Mother's enthusiasm would have been better served had she taken the course herself!

I too have struggled for many years to let go of my sons. Relinquishing control over the small details of their lives has never been easy for me. When my older son was writing all of his school papers in messy, spidery handwriting, I could not resist stepping in. After unsuccessfully nagging him to write more legibly, I finally pushed him into taking typing lessons. At my insistence he reluctantly completed the course. As soon as he finished it, he totally avoided contact with a typewriter for two years.

We are often hardest on the child who reminds us of ourselves, as Angela Barron McBride expresses so poignantly in *The Growth and Development of Mothers:**

> I expect my children to be like me, ONLY BETTER. I want them to be disciplined and steady in their work habits, even though I work in spurts. I tend to complain and indulge in tears when I am hurt, but I expect my children not to whine or tattle on their friends. I am prejudiced about all sorts of things, but I expect to raise daughters who are free of bias. . . . I seduce my friends with cocktails and dinner, but I resent it when my child "buys" a friend's attention with apple juice and animal crackers.

Learning to let go is one of the toughest challenges facing any parent. When my younger son was in fifth grade, he was having a terrible year both socially and academically. He complained that the kids were mean to him; he did not

*Angela Barron McBride, *The Growth and Development of Mothers* (New York: Harper & Row, Perennial Library, 1974), p. 59.

bring home his books because they were "too heavy." I found myself growing angrier and angrier. I saw him as an extension of myself and, since he was "my" son, he made me look bad. I saw both of us as failing. I will never forget what Alice Ginott said when I complained about his self-defeating attitude: "Nancy, if only you could see him as a boy who is struggling rather than somebody who is trying to make your life miserable. If you could only say to yourself, 'Look what this person I love is going through. How hard it must be for him to sit in class, dreading that the teacher will call on him or worried that no one will sit with him at lunch because he's new in school.' "

That statement was a turning point; it enabled me to take Todd's behavior less personally. My anger began to be replaced by empathy as I tried to become his ally, not his constant critic. As a practical solution, I found a high-school junior who taught him how to develop better study habits. She helped him get his motor started far more successfully than all my former carping. After a few years Todd began to appreciate and enjoy school, but those were hard years for both of us.

"A Sweater Is Something You Put on When Your Mother Is Cold"

Meg and her family were about to go out for the afternoon:

Mom: Did you brush your teeth?
Meg: Yes.
Mom: Did you go to the toilet?
Meg: No.
Mom: Do it now so you won't have to go later.
Meg: Okay, okay.
Mom: Put your sweater on. You don't have an undershirt under your blouse and you might be cold.

Meg: No, I want my belt to show.
Mom: But you'll be cold.
Meg: No, I won't.
Mom: Well, I know you. If you're not warm enough, you'll
          be complaining.
Meg: No, I won't.

A familiar refrain? Most of us have spoken lines like these many times, thinking we were being helpful. Far from appreciating our concern, children find such questions and advice intrusive. Some become defiant: "Leave me alone. Get off my case." Others conclude that they are inept: "Mom doesn't think I am smart enough to keep warm. She must be right."

One way to deprive children of a sense of competence is to do more for them than is necessary. To foster responsibility and self-reliance we need to do less, not more. Often we are not even aware of how much we do for our children and how much they could do for themselves if we gave them a chance. One way to find out is to make a list of everything you do for your child in the course of a day, then consider which items you could eliminate. A mother who had great difficulty allowing her seven-year-old to do things for himself made the following list:

Wake him up.
Lay out his school clothes.
Make his breakfast.
Make his lunch and put it in his backpack.
Remind him to brush his teeth.
Brush his hair for him.
Get his jacket out of the closet.
Deliver his forgotten homework to school.
Hang up his jacket when he comes home.
Get him a snack.

Find his karate stuff.
Run his bath.
Do his homework with him.
Pick up his toys and books.
Put his books and homework in his backpack for the next morning.
Put his dirty clothes in the hamper.

When she read her list at one of my workshops, some of the other parents commented that her son could surely do many of these things for himself. One parent added, "You're doing so much for him that he'll always expect such service. He'll never find a wife to do all that."

"That's what I'm hoping!" laughed his mother.

"Good Taste Is What Your Mother Likes"

Maria's mother came to a workshop frustrated by constant hostile confrontations with her twelve-year-old daughter. She described this typical scene in a department store. Maria selected three pairs of pants to try on.

Maria: Aren't these super?
Mom: Try these on. *(Handing her a different pair.)*
Maria: No, I like these better.
Mom: You do? They're horrible. They're sloppy-looking. Put them back.
Maria: No. Just hold them for me.

Mom followed Maria into the dressing room with another pair.

Mom: These are nice. Try them on.
Maria: I don't know.
Mom: What do you mean, you "don't know"? Take those black ones off. They're cheap-looking.
Maria: Where are the ones I picked out? The ones I asked you to hold?
Mom: I put them back.
Maria: What! Why?
Mom: They were awful. You're not getting them.
Maria: Then I'm not trying on anything else. Let's go home.
Mom: Oh, you spoiled brat. You're not getting anything. You don't care what you look like. No daughter of mine is going to wear clothes like that. I'm willing to buy you the best clothes and all you want is junk!
Maria: Forget it! I don't want anything from you anyway.

After looking closely at her words, Maria's mother realized that she was denying Maria the right to her own taste. Her denigrating remarks sent Maria the message: "My acceptance of you is conditional on your being like me." As Maria approached adolescence, her mother needed to step back and recognize her daughter's separateness. A teenager's primary task is to discover who she or he is apart from us.

Haim Ginott told the story of a young man shopping for

his first suit. He said to the salesman, "If my father likes it, can I bring it back?"

New characters, new script: Jessica's mother brought home two dresses for Jessica to try on because she didn't know which one would look better for the eighth-grade graduation. Jessica liked one and her parents, naturally, preferred the other:

Mom: I really like the linen one better. It fits so well.
Jessica: But I love the organdy one.
Dad: Why can't you listen to your mother? She's right.
Jessica: If I have to wear that frumpy linen one, I won't go to graduation at all.

Jessica began to weep and ran to her room. A short while later her mother knocked on the door:

Mom: Jess, I've been thinking about it. You can keep whichever dress you want.
Jessica: Really?
Mom: Yes. You're the one who'll be wearing it, not I. It's time I stopped making so many decisions for you.
Jessica: Thanks, Mom. I love the organdy dress.

Ruth had taken most of her day off to shop for her nine-year-old son Greg who accompanied her through the packed aisles of sale shoppers. When she selected a blue winter jacket, he did not object, but the next morning she realized she hadn't given him a chance to say what he thought.

Mom: It looks like a warm day.
Greg: Good, I can wear my red jacket. You said I could wear it when it is a nice day.
Mom: But the red one is a summer jacket. This is November.
Greg: But you just said it's going to be warm today.

Mom: But it doesn't have a lining.

Greg: I like the red jacket. It's my favorite. It has a lot of pockets. I promise I won't be cold.

Mom: But you look so nice in the new blue jacket that we bought yesterday. It's a bomber jacket, the kind all the boys are wearing.

Greg: I don't care. It's too puffy. I don't like the way it looks in front.

Ruth was about to counter with a string of arguments: "But you let me buy it. We waited in a long line to pay for it. I gave up my only free day to take you shopping. Why did you let me buy it if you didn't like it? . . ." But she stopped herself:

Mom: If you really want to wear the red jacket, you may.

Greg: *(putting it on)* I look so cool. I look thin in this jacket.

Seeing how pleased he was, Ruth realized for the first time how self-conscious Greg was about his weight. From then on she decided to let him have more say in selecting his own clothes.

In my workshops many parents feel strongly about choosing their children's clothing and others let their children make their own choices, within reason (see p. 135). I prefer to give children more latitude in this area because, to me, dictating what children wear interferes with their self-image and autonomy. But each parent has to decide for himself or herself.

Many parents have even more trouble letting go about food issues because most of us have firm ideas about what and how much children should eat. But meals are another area in which giving children more autonomy makes them feel better about themselves and avoids a lot of unnecessary confrontation.

Brandon:	What's for dinner?
Mom:	Lamb and peas and potatoes.
Brandon:	I knew it would be another awful dinner. You know I hate peas.
Mom:	Well, you don't have to eat them all. But you have to eat some.
Brandon:	I hate peas.
Mom:	You must have a vegetable every day.
Brandon:	I'll have one tomorrow.
Mom:	You must have peas today. Even if you don't eat a lot, you must eat some.

We know where this dialogue is headed. How crucial is it that seven-year-old Brandon eat his peas? In the long run, is it not more important that Brandon have the opportunity to have a say about what he chooses to put in his own stomach? If it's important to you that he eat a vegetable, you can give him a choice—peas or carrot sticks; raw or cooked.

Marcy, a slender child of five, was a fussy eater. She and her mother had constant fights about how much she should eat, with Mother urging her to eat more and Marcy protesting that she was full. Her mother decided to take another approach:

Mom:	You know, Marcy, we have so many battles about food. Maybe I make some of your portions too large. Would you like to try something different? Since it is your stomach, you eat as much or as little as you want to, and I'll try not to nag you. Okay?
Marcy:	*(incredulous)* Okay.

The next morning Mother gave Marcy a slice of French toast. Marcy ate three bites, stopped and looked for her mother's reaction.

Mom:	Are you finished? *(A question she had never before asked.)*
Marcy:	Yes.
Mom:	I guess you know better than I when you've had enough.

Marcy looked relieved and put her dishes in the sink. Their mealtime arguments decreased as Mother gave Marcy more control over her food portions. It didn't mean they never again disagreed about food, but Mother began to realize that Marcy was healthy and active in spite of her slenderness. As Mother recognized that Marcy was capable of deciding just how much food she needed, Mother began to back off.

Nine-year-old David's mother grew weary of her son's complaints that "there's never anything good in my lunch." She decided to let him plan his own lunches. "Here's a piece of paper. You have six weeks of day camp with five days in each week to pack a lunch. If you'll make a chart of what you want each day, I'll be able to shop ahead and have what you like. The only rule is: lunch has to be more nourishing than a bag of potato chips." Once given options, David stopped complaining, and as it turned out his lunch choices were reasonably healthy.

As we try to give our children more opportunities to become independent and separate, we may get some mixed signals from them. Children want to make their own decisions but they also want our input. This contradiction is natural—a child isn't ready to leap to complete independence in one step. When your child requests your advice and then rejects it, it is helpful to be flexible and to keep a sense of humor:

Josh:	Will you check my homework?

Mom: Sure . . . But there are three wrong answers to these
         multiplication problems.

She began to rework the problems.

Josh: That's not how the teacher told us to do it.
Mom: Then do it the way the teacher showed you.
Josh: If I get them wrong, then it's your fault.

Josh, and his mother argued about the problems for a few
more minutes. Totally exasperated, Josh declared, "If you
were a teacher in my school, the principal would fire you."
    Instead of becoming defensive or angry, his mother real-
ized that her "help" was no help at all. This matter was
between Josh and his teacher. She resorted to humor. Reach-
ing her arms high over her head, she said, "Please, God, give
me the strength never to interfere with Josh's homework
again." She and Josh both laughed. He took his incomplete
math problems back to school the next day and asked for his
teacher's help. When Josh's mother related this incident, she
commented, "I'm trying to get less involved with his homework because I see that the more *I* worry, the less *he* does."

    When you get contradictory signals from your children,
you may say to yourself, "If they ask for my help, why don't
they accept it?" A child may genuinely want your advice but
when she hears it, she may perceive herself as inadequate
and you as the "expert." A child may say to herself, "If Dad
knows a lot, then I don't know very much" or "Why didn't
I think of that? I must be pretty dumb." Our well-intentioned
answers may increase our children's reliance on us instead
of on themselves, particularly in the case of teenagers. So
what can you do when children seek your advice yet seem
allergic to it? You can let them know that you have faith in
their ability to decide what's best for them. In an attempt to
give eleven-year-old Seth more autonomy, his mother tried this:

Seth: Should I take a shower or a bath or skip both? I have a lot of homework and there's a TV program I want to watch at nine.

Mom: That's up to you.

Seth: Why can't you decide. Gimme a break. I'm only a kid.

Mom: Nobody knows better than you how much time you need. Think about it. I'm sure you can come up with a good answer for yourself.

Seth: Okay. I think I'll take a quick shower.

A decision to shower or bathe may sound insignificant but Seth felt more competent for having made his own choice.

All parents want their children to become self-reliant, competent and *responsible*. We usually equate responsibility with taking out the garbage every day, making the bed every morning, setting the table every night. But a truly responsible child has a sense of responsibility that goes beyond daily chores. He knows what to do when things go wrong. When a problem arises, he feels competent to search for options and select the best solution. How do children get to that point? We help them develop inner responsibility by giving them opportunities to make decisions for themselves.

Ever since she was a toddler, Roberta's parents have given her many such opportunities. When she was six and became separated from her mother in a crowded store, she was frightened but, instead of running from one department to another in a panic, she went directly to the manager to ask for help. Roberta does not always make her bed or clean her room, but she knew how to act responsibly in a difficult situation.

Jeremy noticed there was no milk in the refrigerator. Instead of relying on his mother to bring some home, he called her at work:

Jeremy: Mom, do you want me to go to the store so we'll
           have milk for dinner?

Mom: Thanks, Jeremy. I'm glad you noticed. Yes, it
           would be a big help if you'd get it.

When we give children a chance to exercise autonomy they
occasionally astound us. Julie, seven, stomped in from school
and began complaining to her mother:

Julie: That dumb, stupid Robert Wrightsworth stuck
           bubble gum in my hair and I had a terrible time
           getting it out. The teacher even had to cut a little
           bit of my hair. Would you call his mother and
           tell her what he did?

Mom: *(after a long, awkward pause)* Well, dear, I wasn't
           there. And I don't even know his mother.

Julie: Well, I think she should know what he did. If
           you won't call her, would you please ask the school
           for his phone number? I'll call her myself.

Mom was surprised at Julie's willingness to follow through
on her own. She was afraid of being embarrassed by Julie's
call and by the idea that Julie might be seen as a tattletale
by Robert's mother. But she recognized that this was important to Julie so she sent a note to Julie's teacher asking
for Robert's phone number. The next day, Julie brought
home the number and dialed. Her mother could not help
eavesdropping:

Julie: Hello, can I please speak to your wife? . . . Mrs.
           Wrightsworth? This is Julie. I'm in Robert's class.
           I thought you should know that he stuck bubble
           gum in my hair yesterday. . . . Yes, it's out now.
           The teacher had to cut it out. . . . Yes . . . Okay.
           Thank you. Good-bye.

After the call, Julie looked pleased and her mother decided to reinforce Julie's self-reliance.

Mom: Julie, that was not an easy thing to do but you took care of it all by yourself.

Julie: Thanks, Mom.

When we do less for children we give them a great gift: we give them the message, "I have faith in your judgment." But often we do not have enough confidence in children's ability to let them decide what is best for them because we are too busy worrying about their potential mistakes or failures. And sometimes our children are a lot more competent than we give them credit for. We are surprised when they do things well: "I couldn't believe that was John up there on that stage," or "I never thought Sheila could carry off that project," or "The teacher told me Rachel organized the whole debating team—my daughter? She can't even lift a finger to do the dishes."

Adam's parents fought recurring battles with him about getting up on time for school. One evening when the clock was not pressing them, Adam's father raised the lateness issue in order to try to reverse the pattern:

Dad: Adam, we need to talk about the morning routine. It's not pleasant for any of us. What do you think we can do about it?

Adam: Well, I have to get up so early. I'm tired and you always come in and bug me. *I* know I have to get up.

Dad: What can we do about your getting up on time without us fighting?

Adam: I guess I'll have to get up by seven-fifteen. I'll get my clothes out the night before. But please stop coming in every two minutes to get me up.

Dad: It's a deal. You pick out your clothes the night
        before and I'll try to stop nagging.

Adam went right to his room, selected clothes for the next
day and put them on his chair. The next morning his brother
and sister were up and eating breakfast. Adam hadn't
appeared and Dad was tempted to go to his room, but he
waited. Five minutes later, as his brother and sister were
putting on their coats, sounds were heard from Adam's room.
Dad could barely resist calling out, "Hurry up." Four
minutes later, Adam came in, dressed, and wolfed down
his breakfast. " 'Bye" was all he said as he ran for the
school bus. It was the first morning in months without an
argument.
    But what if Adam had missed the bus? Mom and Dad
could not make themselves late for work by going out of their
way to drive him to school, and school was too far for him
to walk. We want children to learn through consequences
whenever possible, but there are times when their consequences become ours. At those times we really have no choice—
we must step in. But when we do have a choice, we need to
use it, and to allow our children to become responsible for
themselves.

    I had a similar experience when my ten-year-old son forgot
his bus pass. He had gotten a ride across town to a point
where he could catch a bus that would take him forty blocks
to his school. When he was dropped off, he realized that he
had no bus pass and not enough money for the fare. He
called me with his only dime. My first reaction was one of
annoyance that I would have to drop everything and run
across town with the pass. Suddenly I realized that I did not
have to do that. I didn't have to rescue him; this was his
problem, not mine.

Todd: Mom, I forgot my bus pass.

Me: Oh.

Todd: What should I do?

Me: I don't know. What do you think you could do?

Todd: *(after a pause)* Well, I guess I could walk.

Me: That's an idea.

It was difficult for me *not* to pull Todd out of his predicament. My "good mother" instinct said that I should help him: if I did not bail him out, he would be late for school. But he needed this opportunity to think of a solution—even if it meant a forty-block walk. The result? He walked the forty blocks and did not forget his bus pass again.

The bus pass incident was a breakthrough for me. Another turning point occurred several years later when my husband, my sons and I took a winter vacation to a sunny island. I couldn't wait to burst into the sun, play tennis and swim. On our first morning I entered the boys' dimly lit room to find them playing poker. The drapes were tightly drawn so I pulled them open.

Me: Look at this gorgeous day! Let's get outside and enjoy it.

Boys: Aw, Mom, close the curtains. It's too bright.

I was about to lecture them about how much money this vacation was costing us . . . we did not come here to sit in a stuffy room and play cards . . . you could do that at home. Then I realized that this was their vacation, too. If they wanted to spend it in a dark hotel room, that was their choice. I went out into the sun. They stayed in, played cards and emerged only for meals. After two days of poker saturation, they finally came out to enjoy the sun and sea. And they did enjoy it because they were ready to.

Toby: I want to cook my own eggs this morning.

Dad: Fine.

Toby put the eggs in the pan, but they quickly burned.

Toby: Oh, Dad, they're scorched.
Dad: I see.

Toby dished the eggs out and began to eat them.

Toby: They're horrible. I think I cooked them too long.
Dad: Maybe. Or maybe the flame was too high.
Toby: I guess I'll have cereal now, but can I try to fry eggs tomorrow?
Dad: Sure, and maybe you can fry two for me, too.

Dad let seven-year-old Toby do something for himself that he had never asked to do before and that he might fail to do well. When Toby did burn the eggs, rather than discouraging him from trying again with a critical remark ("Why didn't you turn down the burner?" or "You should have been more careful"), Dad simply said, "I see." Toby made the connection between overcooking and "horrible" eggs himself. Had his father taken over for him, Toby would have felt inept. Instead he was motivated by this experience to try again the next day.

Cecile expressed confidence in her eleven-year-old daughter by not intervening even when Ginny asked her to:

Ginny: Mom, will you call my flute teacher and ask him to change my lesson from Tuesday to Thursday so I won't have to miss field day on Tuesday?
Mom: You can call him. His number is in the directory.
Ginny: Please, Mom, it's no big deal. Just call for me.
Mom: Honey, it's your lesson, not mine. You can call.

At one of my workshops, Cecile related the outcome of this conversation.

> *"Ginny was very annoyed with me for not calling, but she did eventually call herself. And the funny thing is,*

*that seemed to be a big step for her. Since then she's been
doing a lot more for herself. Several days after that phone
call she asked her classroom teacher if she could take on an
independent project. That was a first for her."*

Doug: Where's my library book? I need it for my Eskimo
        report that's due Monday.
Mom: It must be at school. It isn't here. Didn't you take
        it with you to school this morning?
Doug: No, I didn't. It must be here. You lost it!
Mom: I'm sure it isn't here. I cleaned today and I would
        have seen it.
Doug: I have to have it. Can't you go to school and get it
        for me?
Mom: Why don't you and Bobby ride your bikes back to
        school and get it?
Doug: No. You get it. Please, please. I have to have it this
        weekend.
Mom: *(buying time)* Let me think about it.

A few minutes later:

Mom: Doug, I think it's an imposition for me to go.
Doug: Well . . . All right, Mom, then don't.

Doug did not go back to school for the book but he did write
his report on Sunday evening with the help of the encyclo-
pedia. Mother was amazed, because Doug wasn't hostile toward her and because he managed to write the report without
depending on her. There is no guarantee that a child will
always follow through on his own each time we disengage,
but this time it worked.

    Doug's mother helped by not helping. If she had gone to
school to retrieve his book, she would have transmitted the
message: "This is more important to me than it is to you."
It would have become more her Eskimo report than his. Like

Doug's mother we are naturally anxious about our children's homework, but Doug's mother did not allow her anxiety to prevent Doug from figuring out his own solution to the problem he got into by leaving the book at school.

It sometimes takes great strength *not* to do things for children. We may feel a sense of loss—we feel less needed as we stop selecting their clothes, correcting their homework, making decisions for them. But we ultimately want children to develop the inner resources to trust themselves, to be able to say in a difficult situation, "I think I can find a solution. I could try A, B or C. I don't have to run home to ask my parents what to do."

One mother in my workshop poignantly summed up the process of separation:

> *"Recently I've tried just to listen to my son instead of probing into all his problems and trying to solve them for him. I've let him know that I thought he'd eventually find his own solutions. I've come to realize that a 'good parent' knows when to let go and let her child make his own mistakes, take the consequences and hopefully learn how to correct those errors himself. She knows how to practice 'benign neglect.' It's like becoming an excellent juggler— hard to do but worth striving for."*

8

Sibling Dilemmas

Sibling rivalry is inevitable. The only sure way to avoid it is to have one child.

Most of us have fantasized a peaceful, harmonious home in which our children will love each other, be thrilled to have a playmate and enjoy each other's lifelong companionship. We may have even chosen to have more than one child to provide that companionship for our firstborn. But when the older child hits the new baby for the first time or shouts, "I hate you, you dummy—I wish you'd drop dead," we are shocked at the hostility. If we can't give up our expectations that our children will always get along well, we are in trouble. Sometimes when we try to suppress the rivalry we unknowingly establish a pattern of denying our children's feelings about their siblings. "You should love him because he's your brother. . . . Your little sister is so sweet to you, why do you always have to be nasty to her?" When we fall into the role of arbitrator, middleman, referee, settler of every petty dispute, we unknowingly increase the rivalry. We take sides and blame one child for "starting it."

Russ, nine, ran to his mother:

Russ: Mom, Mom, Dick punched me in the stomach.
Mom: Can't I leave you alone for two minutes without your attacking each other? Who started it this time?
Russ: He came in my room.

Mom: Dick, stay away from him and you won't get into trouble.

Dick: You're such a crybaby. I hate you, Russ.

Russ: You started it, twerp.

Mom: Stay away from each other if you can't get along.

Dick: I didn't do anything. You always blame me.

Mom: Dick, I know better. Can't you do anything constructive? Stay away from your brother. I don't want you touching each other again!

By asking the question, "Who started it?" Mother was looking for a winner and a loser, as though one child was right and one was wrong. Casting children as "winner" and "loser" only keeps the fight going. Whoever lost this time has to win next time. By attacking Dick ("Can't you do anything constructive?"), Mother aggravated his hostility toward her and Russ. Why should he change his behavior if everyone blames him anyway? In trying to find the guilty party, we are often unaware that our intervention only increases our children's natural rivalry and sets the stage for the next fight.

When children aren't openly fighting or calling each other nasty names, they often are jousting for our love and attention. Each wants to be crowned our "most beloved."

Kitty: Mommy, will you tuck me in first?

Mom: Okay.

Kara: *I* want to be tucked in first.

Kitty: I asked to be tucked in first.

Mom: That's true. She did.

Kara: That's not fair. You always tuck in her before me.

Mom: That's not true. And tonight I'm tucking your sister in first.

Kara: It's not fair.

Kara sulked, Kitty smiled, and Mom left the room frustrated. A similar problem the next day, but this time it was Dad's turn to be in the middle—just where Kitty and Kara wanted him. He and Kara had been grocery shopping and brought home a brownie mix to prepare together:

Kitty: It's not fair. I want to make brownies, too.
Dad: Okay, we'll all do it.
Kara: I want to crack the egg.
Kitty: No. Me. There's only one and I got it first.
Dad: If you two can't decide who's going to crack the egg, I'll crack it myself!

Both protest at that.

Dad: Let's see what else has to be done. Someone needs to measure and pour in water.
Kitty: Me!
Kara: Then I get to crack the egg.

They agree but when it came time to mix, Kara protested that Kitty mixed longer.

When Kitty and Kara's parents relayed these typical sibling struggles at one of my workshops, other parents nodded their heads in recognition. We all agreed about how frustrating, exhausting and repetitive these exchanges are. There are no easy solutions, but if you can accept the inevitability of sibling rivalry and give up your expectations of peace and harmony, you'll be ahead of the game. Your children's rivalry says nothing about your effectiveness as parents, only about the natural competitiveness among siblings.

Caroline had not openly expressed jealousy toward her baby sister, so her parents were unaware of her feelings until they attended Parents' Night and Caroline's teacher showed them her journal. She had written, "Mommy made me give the baby my rattle." Their instinctive reaction was to say, "You are seven years old. What do you need a rattle for anyway? How selfish can you be toward your baby sister?" But on the way home that evening, they talked about how Caroline might well have resented the amount of attention the baby was getting. Her mother put the rattle in an envelope that night with this note and left them on Caroline's pillow:

> *Dear Caroline,*
>   *I now realize that it wasn't right to give the baby your rattle without asking you. I didn't think it meant so much to you. Maybe Santa can bring her one of her own. What do you think?*
>
> > *Love,*
> > *Mommy*

In the morning Caroline read the note, ran to her mother and said, "I love you, Mommy. Thank you for giving me back my rattle."

Once you accept the fact that siblings will be jealous of each other, will vie for your attention and will invariably fight with words or fists, what can you do? The first step is to become aware of their patterns, the next is to stay out of their fights whenever possible and the third is to learn how to intervene effectively when intervention is absolutely necessary.

One way to become aware of your children's squabbling patterns is to keep a "fight journal." This doesn't mean that you must trail your children with a pencil and pad through all their waking moments. But if you try, for even a few days, to take note of when they fight, what seems to ignite the fights and, just as important, when they do *not* fight, you may find some surprising results. After keeping a fight journal for only two days, one mother noticed that her sons, aged six and eight, fought mainly when she was present and less often when they were alone together. She noticed that their motives—whether conscious or not—seemed to be to pull her into the fight and force her to choose sides.

A major benefit of keeping a fight journal is that it puts you in an observer's position, one of neutrality. Instead of jumping in to settle each dispute, this mother stood silently on the sidelines. After keeping her fight journal a few days longer, she noticed that her sons' fights were less frequent and prolonged when she didn't intervene. She awoke one morning to the sound of an argument in the next room:

Corey: You're not coming to my birthday party.

Chris: Oh, yes, I am. I'm coming whether you like it or not.

Corey: Well, if you come, I won't give you any party favors. And if Mom makes me give you a party bag, it'll be empty.

Chris: You're a jerk! You stupid idiot.

In the past their mother would have leaped from her bed to break up this kind of quarrel. But this time she gripped the covers and refused to intervene. Two minutes later the boys were laughing and taking a shower together. She later told my workshop group:

"I realized then that they actually enjoy *these fights. Just the other day Chris asked Corey to play action figures and just to give him the needle, Corey said, 'I can't play action figures because my best friends aren't here.'*

"Chris came back with, 'Oh, come on.'

"Corey replied: 'I'm only kidding.'

"Chris agreed: 'That's right. You're only kidding because you know I'm *your best friend.'*

"I know that they can be best friends at three o'clock and

© 1980 United Feature Syndicate, Inc.

have a huge fight at four, but I've learned that they are far better friends than I'd thought—especially when I don't get involved."

Maggie:	That's mine. You took it.
Alicia:	Well, it was mine to begin with.
Maggie:	*(yelling)* I want it back right now!
Mom:	What's going on?
Alicia:	She took my shirt.
Maggie:	It doesn't fit her anymore. She gave it to me.
Alicia:	I never gave it to her. She's a liar. I want it back!
Mom:	Maggie, give it back to your sister.
Maggie:	You always take her side because she's the oldest. You never agree with me. You like her better than me.
Mom:	That's not so. Now see what you've done, Alicia.

Alicia:	She took what was mine. It's not my fault.
Mom:	Go to your rooms. I'll take the shirt. That way neither of you will have it.

The girls sulked. Mother was disgusted with both of them. No one was satisfied. Trying to play mediator, Mother alienated both daughters.

A few days later she decided to change her approach by staying out of the middle. She overheard them arguing in shrill voices:

Maggie:	Your radio is too loud. I can't hear mine.
Alicia:	The only reason I put mine louder is 'cause yours is so loud.
Maggie:	Turn it down.
Alicia:	No, I won't.
Maggie:	If you don't turn it down, I'll shut it off for you.
Alicia:	You dare to turn mine off and you'll be sorry. Motherrrrr!
Maggie:	Mom, Alicia is bothering me.
Alicia:	She's bothering *me*.

From the next room:

Mom:	I think you two can work this out yourselves.

Mother had decided not to get into their dispute as long as they were not physically hurting each other. When they saw that she was unwilling to jump in as arbitrator, they eventually found their own solution.

Maggie:	I'll turn down mine if you turn down yours.
Alicia:	Okay, I'll turn mine down.

This is not to say that Maggie and Alicia never again argued. But over the next few weeks, as their mother refused to be pulled into their rivalry, they began to work out their fights without her and even fought less often.

Anna and Ron had been fighting bitterly for many years. Their mother usually defended Anna, the younger child, and attacked Ron. This is a pattern many parents fall into: assuming the older one is to blame and siding with the vulnerable, presumably innocent younger child. But the younger one catches on and masters the blame game: she provokes the older child so that he will be scolded. The older one then resents the triumphant younger one. The result: their natural rivalry is intensified by the pattern we help establish.

When Anna and Ron's mother became aware that her involvement was exacerbating the hostility, she decided to try a new, noninterventionist approach. She said firmly, "This quarrel has nothing to do with me. From now on, you two will have to work it out yourselves. I know you can."

Anna glared at her mother the first time she heard this statement. Furious at the idea of losing her staunch defender and ally against her brother, Anna put her hands on her hips and declared indignantly, "What are mothers for?"

Anna soon learned that mothers and fathers are *not* for arbitrating every quarrel. When she and Ron saw that their mother was serious about staying out of their fights, they realized that they had the capacity to settle them. The less you involve yourself as mediator, the greater the opportunities for your children to seek their own solutions.

Sometimes, though, we have to intervene. When children are physically hurting each other, we can't let them "work it out themselves." You can be permissive with a child's feelings, but clear and firm about what is acceptable behavior. You have to keep one sibling from hurting the other not just to protect the victim's safety but to protect the slugger. When he inflicts serious injury on a sister or brother, he feels guilty. He may feel like a "bad child" for harming someone that he (at times) loves. Just as we stop a child from touching a hot stove or running in the street, we need to protect one child from the other—for the sake of both. Sometimes separating them *is* the only solution. One parent found this impartial statement to be particularly useful when her children began to fight: "I will not permit one child I love to hurt another child I love."

There are several ways of intervening without taking sides or escalating their hostility toward each other. You can use skills learned in other chapters, particularly acknowledging feelings and setting clear limits, as Becky and Angus's father did:

Becky: Angus hit me.
Dad: Oh? Angus hit you. I bet that made you mad.
Becky: Yes, and he called me a pig.
Angus: She was bothering me. Tell her to leave me alone or I'll hit her.
Dad: I see that Becky bothers you, but you cannot hit her. We don't hit.
Angus: She hit me. Tell *her* not to hit, then.
Dad: Come here, you two. I am very upset. We have a serious problem. Can you help?
Angus: What?
Dad: You are both breaking the no-hitting rule.
Becky: He hit me first.
Angus: No, I didn't. Shut up, dummy.
Dad: What can we do about this hitting problem?
Angus: I don't know.
Dad: What can we do instead of hitting?
Angus: We can talk.
Dad: Good idea. Instead of hitting, let's remember to talk. Can we all agree to that?
Becky: Okay.
Angus: Okay.

Dad was extremely skillful in this dialogue. He accepted Angus's and Becky's negative feelings about each other without playing judge and jury. In the middle of the dialogue, when another outburst loomed ("He hit me first." "No, I didn't. Shut up, dummy"), Dad did not get sidetracked. He kept the discussion focused on the main issue: the no-hitting rule. He sidetracked Angus and Becky by asking them to solve the problem ("What can we do instead of hitting?"). Dad also realized that teaching values such as no hitting is a gradual process which needs repetition and reinforcement. He didn't expect Angus and Becky never to hit again, but he knew that if he could get them to come up with their own alternatives they would be more likely to accept it than if he ordered them to stop hitting. Instead of issuing a verdict, he remained even-handed, engaged them in mutual problem solving and reiterated a basic family value.

In situations where rivalry is intense, acknowledgment is one of our most valuable tools.

Erica's stepbrother and stepsister were visiting for the weekend. She complained to her mother:

Erica: It's not fair. Dad took Ricky fishing and Linda is with her friends and they won't let me play with them.

Mom: You feel left out, don't you?

Erica: Yes. *(And she burst into tears.)*

Mom: You feel all alone, don't you? I'm alone and I could use a buddy. Would you like to keep me company while I go shopping?

Erica: *(hugging her mother)* Okay, Mom.

This was not a situation in which Erica could be sent back to work out a solution. She needed someone to take care of her feelings.

When Dad was rocking two-year-old Tyler in his lap, Andrea, six, stomped into the bedroom and said, "You never do that to me." A normal response would have been to explain the facts or deny the feelings: "Of course I do. I've been rocking you since you were a baby." Instead, Dad recognized Andrea's feelings.

Dad: You want me to rock only you.
Andrea: Yes.
Dad: You wish Tyler weren't here.
Andrea: I HATE Tyler. If he was a plant, I'd throw him out the window.
Dad: It sure is a problem having to share me with him.
Andrea: I don't want to.
Dad: I know. But you're my only special Andrea.

She gave him a wide, toothless grin. Andrea's father did not try to explain to her that Tyler was just a baby. Instead, he gave Andrea what she needed at that moment: attention, not a lecture. He let her express her feelings of jealousy without making her feel bad. He helped her feel unique by saying, "But you're my only special Andrea."

Ilene brought her six-month-old baby along when she picked Richard up from nursery school. As they were leaving, a group of little girls gathered around the stroller and made a fuss over the baby. Two teachers joined in, and the baby gurgled, cooed and smiled. Richard stood by silently, clinging to his mother's skirt. When the crowd dispersed, waving good-bye to the baby, Richard spoke fiercely:

Richard: I am very mad.
Mom: You didn't like all those people making a fuss over the baby.
Richard: No, I didn't. Not at all.
Mom: It's hard when everyone pays attention to her and no one pays attention to you.
Richard: Yes, and I am very, very mad.

Mom:	You don't think she's so cute.
Richard:	*(vehemently)* No.
Mom:	It's hard on you, darling. Everyone always makes such a fuss over babies.

As she gave him a hug which he returned, she could feel his tension easing.

When we were children, many of us may have heard such statements as "You should be happy for her; she's your sister" or "Don't be silly, everyone made a fuss over you, too, when you were a baby." But Richard's mother was sensitive to his legitimate anger at being ignored. Most of us sympathize with a child whose sibling is in the spotlight but we may be at a loss for words to comfort the child who is left out. Richard was fortunate to have a mother who so eloquently acknowledged his emotions.

We sometimes think that if we treat each child fairly and equally—and make them see that we're being fair—they will stop arguing about who gets more, who gets something first, who's our favorite. But, as hard as we try to be fair, we can never succeed. Even if we believe we're completely fair, children will never agree with us. Since no one wins the fairness game, the best thing to do is avoid playing it. If you don't drop out of the game, you will play right into your children's hands, as Robbie's mother did:

Robbie:	No fair, Reed saw the ice show twice and I only saw it once. You have to get me tickets when I'm better.
Mom:	Don't tell me what I have to do. It's not my fault you have chicken pox. No one is to blame.
Robbie:	I don't care.
Mom:	How many times have you been to the circus?
Robbie:	Twice.

Mom: How many times has Reed been?

Robbie: Once.

Mom: *(now deeply enmeshed in the fairness game)* No, he has never been to the circus. Now let's drop this nonsense.

Robbie: You're not fair. You're mean. You don't care how I feel.

As long as Robbie's mother kept trying to treat each son equally, her children continued to keep score. As long as the scorekeeping goes on, one is always ahead and the other behind—or, according to one, the other is always ahead—and both are trying to catch up.

If you give one child a book and the other asks, "How come you brought her one and not me?" you can simply acknowledge the feeling: "You would have liked me to bring you one, too. You know, sweetie, the next time I see something that seems just perfect for you, maybe I'll surprise you with it." We may not be able to eliminate sibling scorekeeping but we don't have to encourage it. If we participate in the fairness game, our children may take it to the point of absurdity:

Bette, twelve, had just returned from visiting a friend for the weekend.

Bette: What TV programs did Simone watch over the weekend?

Mom: She watched "The Hobbit" earlier this evening.

Bette: What did she watch yesterday?

Mother: She watched "The Jeffersons" last night.

Bette: Did she watch "Operation Petticoat"?

Mother: Yes, she did.

Bette: What! How come? You know she isn't allowed to watch it. You know that's not on our list of programs. I didn't watch it and I think now I should be allowed to watch it next Saturday and she shouldn't.

Mother: Bette, the reason she was allowed to watch that program was that she watched no TV at all Friday night or Saturday morning. Therefore, I stretched the rule a bit.

Bette: Well, I watched no TV either all weekend and so now I should be allowed to watch "Operation Petticoat" next Saturday and she shouldn't.

Mother: No, Bette, it doesn't even out that way. You aren't going to watch "Operation Petticoat" next Saturday and cause all kinds of arguments by doing so. I won't stand for it.

Bette: *(raising her voice)* I want to, and I should be allowed to.

Mother: *(screaming)* Why is it that you aren't home twenty minutes before a problem is created and you find something to complain and argue with me about? I just don't understand you.

Mother walked out and slammed the door.

In *Your Second Child*, Joan Weiss eloquently discusses the futility of the fairness game by saying:

> Although children say they want total equality, it is impossible to achieve, it is a hardship on parents (did you ever try counting the number of sprinkles on two ice cream cones, or the number of Cheerios in two bowls of cereal?) and it is not what the children really want anyway. . . . Research has shown that a policy of providing two sisters two of everything—two swings, two sandboxes . . . two tricycles, two pairs of similar galoshes— does not prevent rivalry. The reason is that children are not really fighting over the swings, or the cookies, or the Jordache jeans. What they are fighting over is

your love. What they need is the reassurance that they have it.*

Rather than aim for complete fairness, you can try to treat each child as *unique* rather than equal. If you give one child a two-wheeled bike for his eighth birthday, you don't have to give each younger one a two-wheeler on his or her eighth birthday. If one child takes piano lessons, the other doesn't have to follow suit. She may prefer guitar, ballet or gymnastics. How boring it would be if children were alike in temperament, talent and looks. Each is different and each evokes a different response in us, making us different parents to each child. One may remind you of your own weaknesses, another may remind you of your spouse's. We treat the second child differently from the first, the third differently from the second. It's easy to fall into the trap of trying to treat children equally, but that is unnecessary as well as impossible. In one of my workshops a mother recalled how her parents gave her and her younger sister the same gifts, privileges and responsibilities:

"We always had to go to bed at the same time. I could never stay up later even though I was older. And when I finally was old enough to wear lipstick, they let her wear it, too," she said. "I deeply resented it—and her—for years."

Why shouldn't an older child have a few more privileges than a younger one? When Jonathan asked his father, "How come Roger can stay up till nine and I can't?" instead of saying, "Because you're only six," Father said, "I bet you can't wait until you're eight and can stay up as late as he does." Dad's response gave Jonathan something to look forward to rather than putting him down because he was younger.

When her children asked her which one she loved the most,

---

*Joan Weiss, *Your Second Child* (New York: Summit Books, 1981), p. 190.

one mother said, "Loving my children is like loving the fingers of my hand. You are all different but I need all of you and can't do without a single one."

Sometimes a little time alone with each child goes a long way. Each child wants our undivided attention, but a sibling usually barges in. A technique that emphasizes children's uniqueness and diminishes the constant demands siblings make on our limited availability is "special time," a specific, designated time when you can play, or read, or talk, or take a walk—and not be interrupted by another child. If you can set aside just ten minutes a day, or every other day, to be alone with each child, you can make them feel special. Some parents take the telephone off the hook during special time because it guarantees no interruptions. When you make special time a predictable daily event, you give children something to look forward to. They know that there is a time when you will focus solely on them and they will compete less for your attention. And when two or more children are pulling at you at once, you can stop and say, "Let's talk about this during our special time."

Vera, a working mother of six-year-old twins, found special time particularly valuable as a way of dealing with her children's intense rivalry for her time and attention. During time alone with Gwen one evening, they were talking about likes and dislikes:

Mom: What's one of your favorite things?
Gwen: My birthday.
Mom: And what's one of your least favorite things?
Gwen: When Margo gets all your attention.
Mom: Sounds like you'd like to have me all to yourself.
Gwen: I'd like to get rid of her sometimes and push her out the door.

Mom: You'd like to be alone with me all the time?
Gwen: No, just sometimes I want to.

Special time gave Gwen the opportunity to express her feelings, and her mother acknowledged them skillfully. Time alone with a parent lets a child feel, briefly, that she is the only child and it fosters a special intimacy. At that time, she doesn't have to share you with anyone else.

In addition to treating children uniquely rather than equally and acknowledging their feelings toward siblings, you can also handle sibling dilemmas with a method I call the "amplifier technique." When siblings are quarreling and dumping their complaints about each other in your lap, you amplify by repeating their accusations and allow them to tell their stories without your taking sides. Edward and Liz's father tried it:

Edward: Liz kicked me.
Liz: No, I didn't.
Dad: Liz, Edward says you kicked him.
Liz: No, I did not.
Dad: Ed, Liz says she didn't kick you.
Edward: She did so.
Dad: Well, kicking isn't permitted around here.

Edward then began pulling at Liz's doll.

Liz: Don't touch my dolly.
Edward: (*screaming*) I want it.
Liz: You can't have it. It's mine.
Dad: Liz, Edward would like to hold your doll.
Liz: He can't. It's mine.
Dad: Edward, Liz says you can't have it. Can you two work it out for yourselves?

To Dad's amazement, three-year-old Edward actually heard his father's words, "work it out."

Edward:	Liz, can I have your doll for a minute?
Liz:	(*holding the doll triumphantly over her head*) No. It's mine.
Dad:	Ed, maybe when Liz is ready, she'll let you hold it.

Liz looked at Dad with surprise. A few moments later she offered Edward the doll. Amplifying each child's demands ("Edward says you kicked him . . . Liz says she didn't kick you") keeps us from siding with one against the other. It encourages brothers and sisters to address each other directly instead of expecting us to settle their squabbles.

Just as we expect our children to love each other, we also expect them to share. But sharing means getting less. Dad's statement ("Maybe when Liz is ready, she'll let you hold it") was very helpful; it not only made Liz feel she had a choice in the matter, but it also expressed his faith in her ability to share—something that is never easy for children. A child may be totally uninterested in a toy until another child makes it irresistibly attractive by playing with it. No child likes to share special toys, candy or the attention of parents. Children become more resistant when we force them to share. Rather than saying, "You have to share with your brother," many parents have found that a more helpful statement is one that stresses the difficulty of sharing: "It's not easy to share. I know. But when you're finished, you can give Jennifer a turn."

You can also encourage children to share more willingly if you add a dash of fantasy to your acknowledgment of the difficulties of sharing, as Naomi and William's mother did. She defused a conflict and kept herself from being drawn into their argument when Naomi, eight, grabbed the last jelly bean from William, four:

| William: | (*jumping up and down*) I want it. I want it. |

Mom:	You wish you had a thousand jelly beans.
William:	Yes, a thousand!
Mom:	All the jelly beans in the world!
William:	Yes, and next time, I want my own bag. I don't want to share with her.
Mom:	Well, we don't often buy candy. But next time we'll count out all the candies and each of you can have the same number. If there's an odd one left, I get to eat it!

Parents in my workshops have used a number of techniques to help children handle their natural rivalry with brothers and sisters. Several parents have run for the tape recorder as soon as a fight breaks out—"Wait! Hold it! I want to get every word down on the tape. Hold the punches till I get it turned on." That often throws a wet blanket on the fight because children become distracted by the tape and self-conscious about screaming at their siblings and hearing themselves replayed. Using a tape recorder is a diversionary tactic that changes the mood, but it won't work if it is used too often.

Other parents have brought out pencil and paper whenever a particularly nasty fight erupts—"Let's write this down. Here, Sallie, jot down all the things you think Ethan has done to you and, Ethan, you write down your complaints about Sallie." Again, the squabble is defused, the children are distracted and you aren't drawn into the middle to play judge.

When Amanda, eight, became furious with her brother for interrupting her playtime with a friend, Mother suggested that she put her feelings into words. She scrawled the following note:

> *Dear Stupid Richard,*
> *How are you? I hope your not fine. You know what would*

make me happy? If I cud punch you in the nose, let it
bleed and brake your teeth. Then I kick you, kill you and
I will be happy.

> *Yours untruly,*
> *Anonymouse*

Amanda never delivered the note. The act of writing it helped
her vent her feelings and later that afternoon she played
happily with "Stupid Richard."

Some parents use paper and crayons for the same purpose,
particularly if their children are too young to write—"If you
are so mad at Ted, why don't you draw an angry picture of
him?" Some children draw pictures of the offending sibling
and then tear up the picture, a perfectly harmless but effective
way of expressing their rage.

Other parents suggest that their children punch pillows
when they're angry with a sibling. Ian and Trudy's mother
bought Trudy an inexpensive inflatable punching bag for her
to sock when her little brother got her goat. When Ian, two,
ripped her coloring book one morning, Trudy, five, an-
nounced, "I want it back and I want it in one piece." But
instead of pummeling Ian, she marched to the punching bag
and gave it several strong swats. Thirty minutes later, before
leaving for school, she kissed Ian good-bye. At another time,
when he was "ruining Castle Grayskull," she again took out
her anger on the punching bag. To reinforce this acceptable
way of expressing hostility, her mother commented, "I notice
that you know just what to do when Ian makes you mad."
This might not work for every child, but almost anything is
worth a try.

As difficult as it is to watch our children argue, throw a
punch and vie for our attention, it is comforting to know that
there is a positive side to sibling rivalry. It may seem difficult
to believe when you hear them screaming at each other, but

sibling relationships give children the most valuable practicing ground for getting along with other people. Fighting with a sibling in the safety and security of their own home gives children a place to learn to "fight clean," to negotiate a conflict, to resolve differences, to realize that life may not always be fair. (Someone has to be the first to be tucked into bed or the only one to crack the egg or to be rocked in Daddy's lap).

Sibling relationships also give children an opportunity to experience—and, we hope, express—a range of emotions. We are sometimes amazed at the contradictory feelings they have for each other. One minute they despise each other, the next they are playing happily or giggling over a private joke. Siblings do have varying and intense emotions toward each other. While we notice the arguing and jealousy more often, probably because they are more loudly expressed, we sometimes fail to notice our children's deep affection for each other. The next time they are screeching at each other, and you are trying your best to stay out of it, keep in mind that this ambivalence is normal and that their relationship will shift over time. The only constant is change! A nine-year-old sister and a twelve-year-old brother may have little in common and much to bicker about, but within a few years they may grow much closer as mutual adolescent interests unite them.

Several parents express surprise at discovering that squabbling siblings actually love each other. Virginia's parents had been deeply troubled by her hostility toward her younger sister; they were astounded by a postcard she sent Ava:

Dear Ava,
    What's up? How are you doing? I can't wait to get home and see you. Can we get into a fight when I get home? Love ya, miss ya, see ya.

                                Love and X X X,
                                Virginia

When we start to get too overwrought at the nastiness between siblings, a note like Virginia's reminds us that anger doesn't eliminate love. In sibling relationships, love and anger coexist.

Robin's mother had frequently noticed how envious five-year-old Robin was of her younger sister. She was pleasantly surprised at the outcome of this dialogue:

Robin: Who do you love more, me or Rachel?
Mom: I love you both.
Robin: Yes, but who do you love the best?
Mom: *(buying time)* What do you think?
Robin: *(whispering)* I think you love me more, but don't tell Rachel. It might hurt her feelings.

Many times we are so preoccupied by children's arguing that we forget that they may even *enjoy* fighting. Fighting is exciting and children hate to be bored. Deep affection can lie beneath the surface. When my sons traded outrageous insults, I discovered that it was just their harmless, unique way of communicating. When Todd, twelve, left a good-bye note for Eric, thirteen, before leaving on a trip, Eric read the note and laughed uproariously. He showed me the note, which was full of insults and obscenities. (At the risk of offending the reader or embarrassing my sons, the content will have to be imagined.) I was shocked, but Eric read it for the true meaning, one of great affection. I learned something important from that note. Even when our children's words sound awful, they do not perceive them as we do. We needn't take their insults too seriously as long as they do not talk that way to others. It is simply sibling-ese.

In helping children explore the range and depth of emotions they feel toward one another, you may need to readjust your expectations. In many families, problems arise because parents expect older children to be in greater control of their emotions (and therefore to behave better) than younger ones. That is a heavy burden. Older children may feel victimized unnecessarily. That is why it is important not to automatically defend the younger and blame the older, but to engage in problem solving.

Derek, four, and Frank, six, hated being apart, but their time together was fraught with bickering and name-calling. When their fights escalated to kicking and punching, Mother separated them, but they soon begged to be together again. Mother decided to ask Frank, her older son, to think of a solution:

Mom: Frank, we have a very serious problem in this house that's disturbing me a great deal.
Frank: I know.
Mom: You do?
Frank: Yes, you're going to say I'm too rough with Derek.
Mom: That's true. I'm really afraid that you're going to hurt him.
Frank: I know.
Mom: Well?
Frank: Now you're going to say "How can we solve this problem?"
Mom: Right!
Frank: I have an idea. We could put two no-hurting notes in the house. One near the door and one in our room. And whenever anyone goes to hurt someone, we can scream, "THE NOTE!"
Mom: What should the note say?
Frank: There is no hurting in our home.
Mom: What a great idea.

Frank and Mom made the notes and posted them. Later that day Derek socked Frank.

Frank: Mom, Mom, I thought of everything except I forgot
that Derek can't read! What should we do?

Mom smiled and took Derek by the hand to the note. She
slowly and solemnly read it to him. Not only did she give
Frank a chance to participate in finding a solution, but she
also demonstrated the seriousness of the no-hurting rule to
Derek and she showed Frank that the rule was as important
for his younger brother as it was for him. The note diminished the fighting, at least for a few weeks. After it lost its
excitement, Mother had to try a new ploy.

Once you recognize siblings' anger, jealousy and love as a
natural range of emotions, you can also help your children
understand that those conflicting feelings are normal and
acceptable. They can love and hate their sisters and brothers
at the same time. When you guide them toward resolving
their differences, coming up with their own solutions and
expressing their feelings for each other, you are preparing
them for future adult relationships.

1982   JOHN R. CASSADY

*"I practice violin partly to please my mother and partly
to drive my sister up the wall."*

The sibling connection is life's longest. You can support siblings' positive feelings and help them cope with the negative ones. When siblings demonstrate caring and affection, you can reinforce them, as Danny and Mark's mother did when Danny, three, was cranky and Mark, six, offered to find his brother's favorite blanket:

Mark: Don't cry, Danny. I'll get your blanket for you.

When he brought it to Danny:

Mom: What a thoughtful thing you did, Mark. Danny is lucky to have a brother like you who thinks about his feelings.

And when those sibling interactions are not so loving, you can also accept children's negative feelings without condemnation; if you do, an envious or angry sibling can accept his emotions without guilt and can learn to develop a loving relationship. A mother in one of my workshops recalled how skillfully her own mother handled such a situation:

"I was about eight and my brother Tom was three when Mother brought home the new baby, Suzie. Tom was extremely jealous. I was in the hall with Mother when we heard a crash followed by the baby's screams. Tom had upended the bassinet and dumped Suzie.

"Mother carefully picked up the baby, soothed her gently and brought her to Tom, who was speechless with fear. I watched with amazement as Mother put Suzie in Tom's arms and said,

" 'Tom, Suzie is very tiny and helpless. You are big and strong and she will need you to protect her for many years to come. I know that I can count on you to be very gentle with her.'

"Tom listened solemnly and said nothing. He was protective of Suzie for many years, and they are still close. Tom wasn't always kind to Suzie, but this was a beginning."

By accepting Tom's jealous feelings without making him feel guilty about them, his mother showed Tom that it is also possible to have loving feelings. Her statement ("You are big and strong and she will need you to protect her . . .") enabled Tom to let his positive feelings emerge.

9

Dealing with the Rest of the World

Making Allies of Other Adults

While I was studying with Dr. Alice Ginott, I ran into an acquaintance whom I hadn't seen in years. As we caught up on lost time, I enthusiastically told her that I was learning how to talk differently to my sons. She looked at me with wry amusement and slight disdain. "You have to *learn how to talk* to your children? You have to *study* to be a parent?" she asked.

Her reaction didn't make me feel defensive because I knew that an enormous change had taken place in my relationship with my sons. After years of being on automatic—of reacting to their behavior with commands, criticism, punishment and nagging—I was thrilled to discover positive alternatives. As I tried to reverse my old patterns, I began to substitute consequences for punishment and praise for criticism. As I learned to acknowledge their feelings and give them more autonomy and less advice, I was exhilarated to see how my discipline skills diminished our power struggles and brought us closer.

But my friend's comments gave me a dose of reality. She

reminded me that many people think that what comes to a parent naturally is good enough. Some may believe that the way to discipline children is to scold, punish, point out their failings. Most people will recognize that the way you speak to children determines how they will respond, but they are not necessarily aware of the need for skill in our exchanges with children.

Reversing your own old disciplinary habits and substituting new responses is difficult enough. You don't need other adults criticizing or challenging you. You need an ally.

When the children began a loud fight, Kathleen's husband threw up his hands, and said, "You're reading all those books about how to raise kids—you should know how to handle this. Why can't you make them behave?"

Kathleen was at a total loss. She had become aware of the dynamics of siblings' fighting and she was attempting to stay out of their squabbles. But how could she win over her husband?

Many parents reach this point. Just as they are beginning to use their newly acquired skills, a spouse, in-law, neighbor, teacher or even a stranger introduces misunderstanding or criticism. At that moment, you may be tempted to lecture the other person on the merits of acknowledging feelings, withholding criticism, giving choices, substituting consequences for punishment. You may want to run through the whole battery of skills you are practicing. You want to scream, "Well, why don't you try doing what I'm doing instead of attacking me?"

Many people who enter in our children's lives are like my old acquaintance; they look upon this business of learning to communicate skeptically. Throughout this book I have been talking about ways to become allies with our children. If you think that's tough, you may find that making allies of your spouse, in-laws and other people is even tougher! If you want to enlist other people as allies—for your sake and for the sake of your children—you can win them over only by demonstrating your skills in action. If you try to convert them by preaching or criticizing their methods, it will only backfire as it did in Seth's family.

At a Passover dinner, Seth, eleven, had been asked by his father to read four questions in Hebrew. Seth read haltingly and as he made more and more mistakes, everyone at the table grew fidgety.

Dad: Seth, it's obvious that you're totally unprepared. You should have practiced. Miriam, you read.

Seth said nothing but fought back tears. The next morning Seth's mother raised the issue with her husband.

Mom: We've talked about this before. You and Seth don't get along very well and what you did last night sure didn't help.

Dad: There's nothing wrong with what I did.

Mom: You embarrassed him in front of all the family and you attacked his self-esteem.

Dad: Well, he should have practiced.

Mom: No one told him to.

Dad: He shouldn't have to be told. No one told me to practice when I was a kid.

Mom: He's not you. I wish you'd listen to me when I try to tell you more helpful ways of communicating with him.

Dad: There's nothing wrong with the way I communicate.

Mom: There are better ways. If you'd just have an open mind and take a course or read some of my books, maybe you'd understand what I'm saying.

Dad: You know I don't have the time.
Mom: If you keep this up, you and Seth are going to be
        enemies by the time he's sixteen.
Dad: You always take his side. When am I ever right?

Mom gave up in frustration when she saw how deadlocked
they'd become.

How could this scene have been improved? Certainly Seth's
mother was correct; her husband's unhelpful words did embarrass Seth. But she might have tried to make an ally of her
husband instead of giving him the same thing he gave Seth—
criticism.

In a similar circumstance, another parent approached his
wife in a more helpful way after this dinnertime scene:

Mom: Anne, you have to clear the table and clean up.
Anne: No, I won't.
Mom: Yes, you will or no dessert tomorrow night.
Mary: *(younger sister)* Remember how well *I* cleaned up last
        night?
Mom: Yes, you are the best girl. Come on, Anne, clean
        up NOW!

Dad watched and listened silently, but was cringing inside.

Anne: N.O.
Mom: If you don't, I'm taking away your skateboard per-
        manently.

Anne eventually cleaned up, but sulked and gave her mother
baleful looks. Later, after the children left the room, Dad
talked to Mom.

Dad: You won the battle but lost the war, dear.
Mom: Well, I got her to clean up, didn't I?
Dad: Yes, but there must be a better way.
Mom: What would you have done?

Dad: Well, I might have asked her for her help rather than threatening her. She reacted the way most kids do in a power struggle.

Mom: I couldn't help it. She's so stubborn.

Dad: I bet you could the next time. I know she can be provocative, but I've seen you get her cooperation before.

Mom: I guess you have a point. I did get her back up by forcing the issue. It's true, when I remember to ask rather than order her, she's usually less defiant.

Even though he didn't approve of his wife's handling of Anne, Dad's words were not an attack. If he had criticized his wife or told her how she should have handled Anne's behavior, Mom would only have reacted defensively. It may sound patronizing, but Dad demonstrated the same skills toward his wife that he had learned to use with his children: he withheld judgment and offered praise; he showed faith in her ability to handle Anne differently in the future ("I bet you could the next time"); he acknowledged his wife's frustration with Anne's behavior ("I know she can be provocative"); and he used a light touch ("You won the battle but lost the war, dear"). He was also sensitive enough to speak to her after the children left the room. When we do have the inevitable run-ins about children's misbehavior, it is important not to attack each other in front of them—playing good parent vs. bad parent:

Dad: *(yelling)* Look at that Play Doh all over the living room! The children have ground it into the carpet and some is even stuck to the wall.

Mom: Raymond, why don't you try some of my new techniques?

Dad: Like what?

Mom: Don't give orders. State facts. Describe.

Dad: Describe? Describe what?

Mom:	Just say "The Play Doh is on the carpet and on the wall. It needs to be cleaned up now."
Dad:	Yeah? And when they are wiping it off the wall with their shirtsleeves?
Mom:	*(sweetly)* Then say, "Now there's Play Doh on your shirt. Can you think of something better to clean it up with?"
Dad:	Oh, yeah. Sounds great! *You* handle it.
Mom:	*(smiling)* All right. Follow me.

They walked into the living room and Mother said calmly, "The Play Doh needs to be cleaned up from the carpet and the wall." The children began to clean up. Mother looked triumphantly at Dad.

Mother may have been skillful with her children but she failed to treat her husband with equal skill. Her superior attitude made Dad more resistant. Instead of trying to make him an ally, she alienated him by stressing her competence and his ineptitude. Her smugness made it impossible for them to work together as a team.

When you are trying out new skills and your spouse, who is not, says, "You're the expert, you handle this," there are several ways to respond without making him or her feel like the outsider:

"I wish I did have all the answers."

"Yes, I've read a lot, but I really feel that I need your help, too."

"Would you read this and tell me what you think?

"I wish I always did know what to do, but I don't."

If you expect your spouse to have identical attitudes about childrearing, you're in trouble. You are each very different people. You had different sets of parents who raised you differently, so you probably have varying expectations of yourselves and of your children. Your child's messy room may drive your spouse up the wall but may not bother you that much. You each have your own strengths and failings. And you need to figure out what is really important to each of you and be prepared to compromise. But you can use your differences to mutual advantage. If one of you is uptight about the children's dawdling in the morning and the other is not, you can agree that the more relaxed parent handle the morning scene and the parent who is less anxious about bedtime oversee that routine. You can be allies without being carbon copies of each other. You don't need to accept the myth that parents must always present a "united front." In the real world it is impossible to be totally in sync and consistent, not only because of our individual differences, but also because we frequently change our minds and our moods. In fact, it can be beneficial for children to see that their parents have a wide range of emotions and points of view. But you also need some unequivocal agreements so the children don't master the divide-and-conquer game ("If Mom says 'no,' let's ask Dad"). We don't want to contradict or undermine one another in front of the children. We can try to work out our differences in their absence.

This book is based on the premise that the way we speak and act determines how children will respond. The same is true of adults. If you use words that encourage others to cooperate with you, instead of blaming them for their shortcomings, you are more likely to elicit the response you desire. If you try this with a spouse, grandparent, teacher, caregiver or anyone else who plays a significant role in your child's life, you may gain an ally who will give you valuable support.

As you practice your new skills, the people you live with every day will see your example. They may resist or simply

Reprinted by permission of Jerry Marcus

"Are you going to believe me, your own flesh and blood, or some stranger you married?"

be unwilling to try your new techniques. All you can do is be a model and hope that they will eventually imitate you.

But what can you do in the meantime? What can you do when your spouse is berating your son, or your mother-in-law is criticizing your daughter's appearance? In many instances, the best you can do is to stay out of it. You don't want to side with one person against the other. You can later say to them individually that you understood how each one felt.

Daryl's grandmother was used to issuing a stream of commands:

"Don't climb on that, you'll fall. . . ."

"Watch out! You're going to hurt yourself. . . ."

"Don't do that, you'll scratch the tabletop. . . ."

Daryl's response to each order, "No, I won't," only increased their tension. It was painful for Daryl's mother to watch her son's discomfort around his grandmother, but she did not want to intervene in any way that might pit one against the other. After some careful thought, she spoke to Daryl while he was brushing his teeth and Grandmother was out of earshot:

Mom: It must be hard having Grammy telling you what to do and what not to do every minute.

Daryl: It is.

Mom: You know, I have an idea why Grammy does that.

Daryl: Why?

Mom: Well, she hasn't seen you since you were four and she doesn't realize that you can stand on the bed without falling and jump down without hurting yourself and pour juice without spilling it. She doesn't know what a capable boy you are now.

Daryl did not comment but seemed to be listening.

The next day Grandmother chuckled as she reported to Mother, "Daryl just told me I didn't have to worry about him so much. He said, 'I'm five now so you don't have to tell me what to do anymore.' " Over the next few days, Mother frequently overheard Daryl say, "Don't worry, Grammy, I won't fall. You don't have to tell me what to do."

This change came about because Daryl's mother avoided criticizing or blaming either Daryl or his grandmother. In speaking with Daryl, she showed him that she was on his side and helped him feel good about himself. If she had said something like, "Please don't run and jump around so much. You have to be less wild around Grammy. You're making her so nervous," Daryl would have felt even more criticized—now his mother was ganging up on him, too. Instead, his mother's skill helped him see himself as capable and he was better able to respond to his grandmother. And his grandmother accepted Daryl's remarks with good humor and curtailed her orders.

Sometimes you don't have an opportunity to speak to your child privately, as Daryl's mother did. You can't help but be caught in the middle, but you can avoid blaming either party or making matters worse:

Grandpa came for Sunday dinner. When the cat pounced onto the table, he shouted, "No" and swatted the cat. Rosa began to cry. "No, Grandpa, please don't hit my cat!" Rosa's father did not have the option of taking Rosa aside and explaining that Grandpa did things differently; Dad had to intercede on the spot. He did so diplomatically: "We don't hit the cat. We put her down and tell her firmly, 'Not here.' " Later the cat jumped on the table again. Grandpa did and said nothing. Rosa looked at him and at her father with wide eyes. Dad took the cat, put her on the floor and said, "Not here."

It is difficult not to be caught between our children and our parents or in-laws, who usually have very different notions about raising children. We want to be on our children's side and, at the same time, we don't want to alienate our parents or grandparents. When Amy's grandmother complained to Amy's mother about her granddaughter's appearance, Mother simply acknowledged Grandmother's feelings:

Mom: You'd prefer it if she wouldn't wear jeans and baggy sweaters. You'd probably like to see her looking more feminine, like when she wore dresses.

Grandmother: I certainly would. She used to look so lady-like.

Mom: I see your point but I think it's important for her to begin making more of her own decisions about things that concern her so I'm letting her pick out her own clothes.

As a major character in your child's life, the teacher is worth trying to enlist as an ally. Unfortunately many parents and teachers approach each other warily. As one teacher said, "Until I became a parent myself, I blamed the parents for everything the kids in my class did wrong."

I can usually tell when parents have just had school conferences in which the teacher has criticized their child. They come to my workshop devastated, angry with their child, angry with the teacher and feeling inept themselves.

Most teachers are dedicated and well-intentioned but not all are aware of the effect they have on parents, particularly if they say something negative about a child. Parents hope to hear wonderful things from their children's teachers. As Ellen Galinsky wrote in her book, *Between Generations:**

> Parents frequently look to the other adults in their children's lives for overt or covert judgment of: how have I done as a parent . . . ? "I remember the first months of school," the mother of a three-year-old says. "I wanted to be told in no uncertain terms that I had a fabulous child who had been raised to be a delight in school . . . I was coming to the teacher for an A-plus in parenthood. She was supposed to give me that A-plus and she didn't. And that hurt . . ." Teachers don't always realize the power of their words. . . . In leaving out the positives or concentrating on what's wrong about a child, a teacher can devastate parents, can in fact shape parents' pictures of their children.

*Ellen Galinsky, *Between Generations* (New York: Times Books, 1981), p. 158.

Teachers who are aware of parents' sensitivity rightly ask, "How can I tell parents about their child's problem behavior?" Instead of using labels—he's sloppy, immature, careless, stubborn, not living up to his potential—a teacher can describe the problem:

"John needs to remember to raise his hand rather than calling out."

"Rachel sometimes fidgets and finds it hard to sit still, but we're working on this together."

"Roger needs help in using words when he gets upset rather than hitting or snatching things from the other children."

Patrick's teacher had branded him "immature," the class clown and "lacking in self-control"—all by the age of five! She called his mother to school for a conference, and Mother dreaded what she might hear. She knew she could easily become defensive, but realized that she had to engage the teacher's cooperation on behalf of her son. At the beginning of the conference, Mother decided to open the discussion by asking the teacher for some positive observations about Patrick. The teacher gave several enthusiastic reports but then reeled off such negative labels as "restless" and "immature."

Labels are subjective, imprecise and open to misinterpretation. They stick to a child like glue and a parent rarely forgets them. Patrick's mother tried not to become defensive or critical of the teacher's casual generalizations. She tried instead to get his teacher to do what she had learned: describe his actions instead of evaluate his character. She asked the teacher for concrete examples of his "immaturity." The teacher was able to be more specific: "At circle time, when all the children are seated quietly, he jumps up and down every two minutes." Once into specifics, Mother and teacher began to discuss practical solutions that might help Patrick, such as praising him each time he sat quietly.

The conference ended with Mother and teacher joined as allies rather than adversaries. A day later Mother reinforced their alliance by writing a note of appreciation:

> *I am happy to see that you are building Patrick's confidence and stressing his positive qualities which I know encourage his good behavior. I really appreciate the time you spent with me yesterday. Please keep in touch with me if there's anything further you would like to discuss or if I can be of any help. Once again, thank you for your interest in helping my son.*

The teacher later remarked to Patrick's mother that it was so nice to receive a positive note because generally she hears only complaints from parents.

One way to promote a better parent-teacher partnership is to include your child in school conferences. When a child is present, a teacher is less likely to use labels. Rather than talking *about* the child, the teacher can address her directly. After all, the child is the only one who can alter her behavior.

Donald, a seventh grader, was late for school so often that the teacher called his mother and asked her to come in for a conference. He showed her the roll book and pointed out that Donald averaged two latenesses a week:

Mother: I think it is important that Donald hear about this directly from you rather than me.

Teacher: Good idea. I'll call him in from study hall now.

When Donald arrived, Mother tried to say as little as possible because she recognized that this was a problem Donald had to resolve. After he and the teacher discussed the reasons for Donald's lateness, they all worked out a plan to help him be on time. As she was leaving Mother said to the teacher, "I want to thank you for including Donald and making him part of the solution. When you described the problem, it made a greater impression on him than all my nagging."

The older the child, the more crucial it is to include her in school conferences. I believe that from about third grade on, it is helpful to have your child available to provide first-hand information. For example, if we meet with a teacher alone and the teacher reports, "Patsy hasn't been bringing in all her homework assignments," we go home and relay that information to Patsy. She is likely to feel that both teacher and parent are ganging up on her. She'll protest: "That's not true." What can we say? Who are we to believe?

Since the child is the only one who can change, she needs to hear and respond to the teacher's comments. To many teachers, the notion of having a child present at a conference may seem more difficult or awkward in what is often an already tense situation. But those who have tried it find it can be a helpful and effective way to gain a child's cooperation and engage her in problem solving.

Twelve-year-old Anthony was shocked when he received a failing notice in gym:

Anthony: Oh, God, I try to do everything the gym teacher wants but he's always taking off points. I hate gym. But I never thought he'd flunk me.

His mother listened and suggested that they meet with the gym teacher. They did meet a few days later:

Mom: Since this concerns Anthony, I think he should be present.

The gym teacher appeared uncomfortable with the idea but Mother persuaded him to give it a try by saying, "Anthony is confused about this failing grade so I'd like him to talk with you since he knows much more about it than I do." At first the gym teacher ignored Anthony and spoke directly to his mother. He launched a lengthy explanation of state and federal regulations, defended the marking system and pleaded that the rule requiring a student to pass gym was "out of my control."

Mom:	I know some things are out of your control, but let's see if we can help Anthony with this situation.
Gym teacher:	Well, that's a good point.
Mom:	Why don't we let Anthony tell us how he feels about it?
Gym teacher:	Good idea. Why do you think you failed gym?
Anthony:	Well, I think I try, but there are some things that I'm really not interested in.
Gym teacher:	Well, Anthony, it's important that you try. But I failed you because you missed too many classes and never made them up.
Anthony:	Oh, that's why you failed me. But I was in the school play and I couldn't make them up because we had rehearsals.
Gym teacher:	You never brought me a note from the drama teacher.
Mom:	Anthony is concerned that this failing notice might keep him from going on to seventh grade.
Gym teacher:	Look, Anthony, I'm sure we can work this out. Now that the play is over, I expect you to make up some of the classes you missed. I'm available every afternoon for extra coaching.
Anthony:	Yeah, that seems fair. I can do that.

Anthony's mother used several skills: first she brought Anthony into the discussion and, even though the gym teacher was uncomfortable, she tactfully encouraged him to include her son. Then she didn't allow the discussion to get mired in "regulations." She kept the issue on track—without criticizing the gym teacher. She directed the discussion toward her son by suggesting he "tell us how he feels." It was, after all, his dilemma. Anthony and the gym teacher communicated directly with each other and clarified their misunderstanding while Mother became a spectator and not a go-between.

Other people who enter your child's life only briefly can be engaged as allies when their support is required to help your child in a troublesome spot. Karen, six, had to visit the dentist. She whined and fussed to her mother on the way. When they arrived at his office, Karen tensed. Her mother prepared for a scene. The dentist finally saw them after a long wait and he spoke curtly to Karen.

Dentist: Now just climb up in this chair and sit still. This won't hurt.

Karen squirmed in the chair.

Dentist: Be still. Open your mouth wide.

Karen clamped her teeth together tightly as the dentist reached for his instruments. Karen's mother could see the scene growing worse.

Mom: Dr. Fisher, Karen is feeling anxious about this. I know you're in a hurry but I think it would be easier for both of you if you could tell her what you're going to do. I'm sure Karen will be more cooperative if she knows what to expect.

The dentist nodded. His tone of voice softened as he showed Karen what instruments he would use and explained just what he would do next. She visibly relaxed and the appointment ended with the dentist thanking Karen for being "such a cooperative young lady."

Would that everyone could interact with children as skillfully as Carla's pediatrician. When Carla, eight, was frightened and apprehensive about having a throat culture, she told her mother she would never let the doctor do one. When they arrived at the pediatrician's office, she cried and screamed. Instead of forcing her to open her mouth, the doctor spoke softly:

Doctor: Carla, I know you don't like throat cultures but I promise I'm the quickest throat culture doctor in town. Just let me give you this one and if I'm not the best, you never have to let me give you another.

Carla: *(stopped crying)* Okay.

Doctor: Great. You can either lie down or sit up. And you can keep your eyes open or closed.

Giving Carla choices made a big difference in her acceptance of the dreaded throat culture. She chose to sit up and keep her eyes closed. It was over quickly and peacefully. When the pediatrician prescribed some medicine, she gave Carla a choice of pills or liquid. Carla was amazed. This was the first time she had ever been consulted during an examination. Mother said to the doctor, "Your way of treating my daughter made this visit a pleasure instead of a nightmare." After leaving the office, Carla told her mother, "I want to go back to that doctor the next time I'm sick."

When we are in the public eye, we feel added pressure to make our children behave so that they reflect well on us. Some children sense our pressure to perform and may deliberately act up to prove, "I'm not your puppet." This adds to our embarrassment. When the eyes of other adults are upon us, it is difficult to keep from reacting self-consciously, especially when we feel we are being judged. Whether others say it or the message is implicit in their stares, we hear, "Why can't you handle your kid?" In these awkward public situations, if we can remember that our child is more important than that stranger glaring at us, we can more easily focus on our child's needs.

You may be mortified when your four-year-old asks embarrassing questions, as Drew did when he and his mother were squeezed into an elevator with an obese man.

Drew: Why are you so fat?
Mom: *(gasping)* Drew . . .
Man to Drew: Because I eat too much candy.

For the rest of the elevator ride, Drew and the man enjoyed a discussion of sweets and they parted with a cordial goodbye. Young children are hardly models of tact. They are immensely curious and outspoken. (As one mother said, "I wish I could teach him to be *selectively* truthful!") Fortunately Drew's obese acquaintance understood this lack of diplomacy. Had he reacted negatively to Drew's comment, there's very little that Mother could have done on the spot. But afterward, she might have said, "Drew, I know you didn't mean to hurt that man, but when you talk out loud about people's looks, it can make them feel bad."

We do have to teach politeness and consideration but we do not want to humiliate our child by pointing out his failings in public. In situations like these it is important to keep in mind that, if we must step in, we need to take care of the feelings of the person who means the most to us—our child.

Jimmy's mother left him in the park with a neighbor for a few moments while she went back home to get his bike. As she returned with the bike, Jimmy, four, ran to her and burst into tears. Through the tears he said something about someone getting hurt. His mother put her arm around him and stroked his head until he was able to tell her the story:

Jimmy: I was playing with a stick and I poked a little kid in the eye. His eye didn't fall out, Mommy, but he's hurt. And he didn't bleed but I'm very, very bad. I didn't mean to, but I hurt him. Oooooooh, Mommy!

And the tears gushed again.

Mom: Jimmy, it sounds like an accident. I know you're not a bad boy. But let's find the little boy and see if he's okay. Where is he?

Jimmy, still weeping, led his mother toward the spot where he'd been playing. Mom could see the child in his mother's lap, but she couldn't see how badly he was hurt.

Jimmy: I want to tell him I'm sorry, Mommy, but his daddy is really mad at me. See, that's him.

Mom then noticed a large man, about six feet six. She immediately guessed that he had spoken harshly to Jimmy and frightened him.

In telling the story later, Jimmy's mother said she was intimidated by the child's father and didn't know how badly the child was injured. But she tried to speak as calmly as she could:

Mom: I understand that there was an accident and that my son Jimmy hurt your son.
Boy's father: My son was using the stick like a fishing pole but *yours* was using it like a sword!
Mom: Well, right now we have two boys who are hurt. Your son's eye is hurt and my son is

	hurt inside and they need us to help them feel better.
Jimmy:	I'm sorry. I didn't mean to hurt him.

And Jimmy started crying again.

Boy's father:	Well, that's okay. I guess it was an accident. I can see you didn't mean to hurt him. I'm sorry I yelled at you.

Jimmy's mother intervened courageously with a stranger. On some occasions we may hesitate to step in on our child's behalf because the person involved is *not* a stranger and it may be awkward to confront someone we know. Eleanor found herself in such a predicament with a neighbor who "came on too strong," as Eleanor explained it. "She was always overly friendly and demonstrative toward my children. One day she saw us on the street, rushed toward us and swooped Carol up in a tight hug. I knew Carol was ill at ease but I was too embarrassed to say anything for fear of being rude."

Eleanor's reaction illustrates the drawbacks of a rule most of us were brought up with—whatever you do, don't offend the other person. (Our own children don't count with this rule!) Because she was embarrassed, Eleanor spared her neighbor at the expense of her child. Eleanor's silence gave Carol the message that it would be unacceptable to tell the woman not to hug her. By saying nothing Eleanor unintentionally taught Carol to ignore her own valid feelings in order to be "nice."

What could Eleanor have said to her neighbor without being offensive? She might have said, "It makes Carol uncomfortable when someone hugs her without asking her first" or "I wish you'd ask her before you do that."

Although Eleanor was uneasy with her failure to intervene at the time, she later realized that she could use the incident to teach Carol how to cope with future situations. That evening:

Mom: Did you feel funny when Mrs. S. hugged you?
Carol: I didn't like it.
Mom: Well, the next time if someone is about to hug or kiss you and you don't want them to, you can say, "Please don't hug me. I don't like it."

You can also prepare your children to deal with awkward incidents by role-playing with them. And you can tell them, "Even when people want to kiss you to be nice, you don't have to let them touch you if you don't want them to." Responses that take children's feelings seriously help them trust their instincts and gain confidence to deal with the rest of the world.

As you acknowledge children's feelings, promote their self-esteem and encourage their autonomy, the rest of the world reminds you daily that it is not in step with your efforts. A father in one of my workshops once questioned:

"How is my child going to deal with others if he gets used to our being so empathic and caring of his feelings? Most people aren't going to talk this way to him. How will he deal with them?"

That is a valid concern. It's true, the rest of the world isn't as understanding as we are trying to be with our children. But I strongly believe that if there is even *one person* in a child's life who sees him in a positive light, who delights in him, who appreciates what is special about him, then that is indeed a fortunate child. Hannah's mother filled that role for her daughter. Even when Hannah made mistakes, her mother saw them as opportunities for learning rather than a reflection of Hannah's lack of competence. When Hannah went skiing for the first time and could not get the hang of it after hours on the beginners' slope, the ski instructor said, "Oh, forget it. You'll never catch on."

Hannah was initially discouraged but instead of giving up, she later told her mother, "I decided to try it a few more times. All of a sudden, it clicked and I got it! I felt so great!"

A child like Hannah who has an empathic person in her life is less likely to absorb negative criticism from teachers, peers, relatives. She sees herself as capable and competent. When criticized, such a child will be able to say, "That says something about them, not me."

10

It's Never Too Late

You Always Get
Another Chance

Ruth used to select all her nine-year-old son's clothing. She spent a whole day shopping for a new jacket for Greg.* But when he rejected it in favor of his old red jacket, Ruth recognized for the first time how self-conscious he was about his appearance. The incident was a breakthrough for Ruth. It marked the beginning of Ruth's letting Greg make his own decisions about clothing. From then on, Ruth told a workshop group, she grew more confident about letting go of Greg. As she gave him more opportunities to make choices in many areas of his life, he became more cooperative and self-confident.

Ruth became increasingly aware of curbing her automatic reactions to Greg's behavior. Instead of *reacting* impulsively, she *responded* thoughtfully. She tried expressing her irritation and anger in words that showed Greg how *she* felt, not how "bad" *he* was. Rather than labeling or criticizing him, she substituted statements about her feelings ("I get furious when I see . . .") The more conscious Ruth became of how unhelpful her old ways were, the more thrilled she was to have a variety of new alternatives.

*See Chapter 7, pp. 142–43.

"Now when I catch myself about to lecture, accuse, bribe or threaten him, I can say to myself, 'Hey, wait a minute. I don't have to do that. I can describe what needs to be done to correct the situation or involve him in solving the problem. I can let a consequence take over instead of punishing him.' And when he's upset or complaining, I'm more able to listen and acknowledge how he feels without blaming him for causing the problem or assuming he's at fault and making him feel worse. Now that I've learned these new skills, I'm amazed at how much more peaceful our homelife is. I can hardly believe the change!"

Ruth was beaming by the time she finished describing her successes. But when the workshop group met again the following week, Ruth appeared downcast.

"I blew it. I really blew it this week. Everything had been going beautifully. I'd been praising everything he did well. I wasn't being so critical. But then on Tuesday, Greg made me so angry. He was roughhousing and broke a vase that belonged to my grandmother. Nothing valuable, but very sentimental to me. And to make it worse, he tried to hide the evidence. I was mad that he broke it and I was more mad that he tried to deceive me. Well, when I saw what was going on, I exploded. All my skills flew out the window. I screamed and raved. It was an awful scene. Is all the good undone?"

Ruth's despair was certainly understandable. Just when she was moving forward with these skills, she crashed. Her fall seemed harder because she had been flying so high.

But, no, all the good wasn't undone. Ruth—and all of us—cannot expect to use these skills successfully all the time. That is not a realistic goal. We need to accept our own imperfections just as, in this book, we have been trying to accept the fact that our children are imperfect and not the angels we may have fantasized they would be. We need to be compassionate with ourselves as well. Sometimes we are just too frazzled, too exhausted, too preoccupied by other concerns. All we can hope to do at these moments is not cause damage to our children and to our relationship with them. As discussed in Chapter 5, after an angry explosion you can exit from the scene to cool off and later talk to your child about how you felt and what made you angry. Despite the flare-up, you can reassure her that you still love her.

Even when you fail to use your new skills, children always give you another chance to practice them—sometimes sooner than you'd like! Tommy's mother thought she was making progress until an evening when Tommy, twelve, hit her where it hurt: he criticized her cooking after she had spent a lot of time preparing a special dish.

Tommy:	What's this stuff all over the chicken?
Mom:	It's a gourmet cream sauce.
Tommy:	Yuck. This looks disgusting. Why can't you make good stuff like Grandma does?
Mom:	Oh, just be quiet and eat. It's delicious. I'm sick and tired of hearing you always complaining, complaining, complaining.
Tommy:	I do not always complain!

For the rest of the meal Tommy poked at his plate, and his mother ate in seething silence, angry with him and equally angry with herself for falling back into her old ways. She knew she had barked a command ("Just be quiet and eat"), denied his perception of the food ("It's delicious") and criticized (". . . always complaining, complaining, complaining").

But Tommy's mother didn't give up on her new skills because she realized that Tommy would soon give her another chance to use them. A few nights later she was serving turkey with gravy. This time she was ready.

Tommy:	What's this gooey stuff?
Mom:	It's mucus!
Tommy:	Ha, ha, ha! It sure does look like it.

Mom: I guess to you it does.
Tommy: I wonder what would happen if they killed tur-
          keys that had colds and they really could have
          mucus on them.

Tommy laughed hilariously and even tried some gravy on his turkey. He didn't give it four stars, but his mother's use of somewhat vulgar humor defused a potential confrontation and enabled them to have a delightful dinner together.

No matter how often you slip and utter uncaring or hurtful words, don't be disheartened. You can always learn from these occasions and try to refine your skills for the next time. You don't have to be at the mercy of habitual, impulsive reactions.

But change of any kind is never easy. And change that involves giving up something that you are accustomed to is particularly difficult. Every new skill requires practice. If you have never ice-skated or played the piano, you are going to stumble and falter many times before you achieve mastery. Even after years of practicing the skills I teach, I had this message brought home to me by my son Eric. I had begun a tirade that was anything but a model of how to talk, when he stopped me in midsentence by saying:

"Mom, I bet you don't tell the parents in your workshops to talk to *their* kids the way you're talking to me right now!"

Of course he was right. And we were able to laugh about it—after I had cooled off.

To "make Kelly behave" her mother used the only disci-plinary tools she knew. She threatened, cajoled, nagged, pun-ished . . . But over time she learned more helpful ways to encourage rather than force her daughter's cooperation. She found that by using different techniques even five minutes more a day, it worked—Kelly became much more respon-sive.

Kelly's greatest fear was a visit to the doctor. She was running a temperature of 104 and her mother called the pediatrician. When Kelly overheard her saying on the phone, "Yes, Doctor, we'll be right over," Kelly ran to her room screaming, "No, no. I won't go. No way. N.O." She slammed the door and hid under her bedcovers.

Mom: I see you are very upset.

Kelly: *(screaming)* I'm not going. You can't make me. I won't go!

Kelly's mother sat on her daughter's bed as she sobbed. Mother said nothing for a while but rubbed Kelly's back. As the cries began to subside:

Mom: I understand that you're worried about what will happen at Dr. Barker's office.

Kelly: I don't want to go.

Mom: I can see that you don't.

Mother said nothing more but thought of how she could engage Kelly's cooperation without force. After a few minutes:

Mom: Honey, when your body is sick, it isn't up to you or me to say we should not go to the doctor. When your body is sick, what we have to do is get it well.

Kelly's cries stopped. She rolled over and looked at her mother.

Mom: It isn't up to you to vote "yes, doctor" or "no, doctor." I have to help you get better. That's my job. I can help make you as comfortable as possible at the doctor's office. You can sit on my lap. I can hold your hand. We can find out what he has to do before he does it.

Silence.

Mom: So, Kelly, let's go see Dr. Barker now.

Kelly: Okay, but will you promise to stay with me the whole time?

Mom: Yes, of course, I will.

A year earlier, Kelly's mother would have threatened ("If you don't come with me immediately, you're going to lose your favorite toys for a week") or she might have shamed her ("You're such a crybaby") or she might have tried a bribe ("If you go with me to Dr. Barker, I'll get you a big chocolate ice cream sundae"). But she was able to avoid the old patterns. She now knew how to use the skill of acknowledging feelings to win her daughter's cooperation ("I see you are very upset . . . I understand you're worried about what will happen . . ."). By responding to Kelly's feelings she showed her daughter that she was on her side. She couldn't eliminate Kelly's dread of the doctor, but she encouraged her to face the ordeal by letting her know that her mother understood her fear and would stand by her.

Kelly's mother didn't have an easy challenge. She knew she must get Kelly to the doctor. She was able to be permissive with her daughter's feelings while, at the same time, setting a clear limit (". . . it isn't up to you or me to say we should not go to the doctor . . . It isn't up to you to vote . . .").

She went even further by bringing in another skill. She gave Kelly several options (within Mother's limit that she must visit the doctor): "You can sit on my lap. I can hold your hand. We can find out what he has to do before he does it." By spelling out those choices, she gave her daughter the opportunity to exercise some control in a difficult situation.

Kelly's mother hadn't always handled tough situations with such success. But each time she blew it, she tried to examine what had gone wrong and to use that information to deal more effectively with the next problem. Many parents, like Kelly's mother, find that one success builds on another. As a result, you begin to see your children in a different light and enjoy them more. It is a snowball effect. When a child feels liked and appreciated, your delight in him is reflected in his behavior.

Kelly's mother may seem too good to be true, but keep in mind that the dialogues in this book are real. Actual parents have spoken these words to their children. This is not a formula book. There are no "shoulds." These dialogues are meant to suggest models, not formulas to be memorized or repeated verbatim. You need to be comfortable about adapting them to your own style. You know your child and what works best for both of you.

The skills we have discussed in this book can reverse generational patterns. As one parent explained, "Although I know my parents meant well, I see that the way they spoke to me only created conflict and resentment. It may have made me obey for the moment, but in the long run it didn't create lasting rapport with them. I want to have a different kind of relationship with my kids."

I believe that you can begin using positive communications skills at any time in your children's lives. Naturally the earlier you start, the better prepared you'll be for their adolescence. And you may get an added bonus—you'll be able to have a closer relationship with them when they become adults. All parents hope that their grown children will want to spend time with them out of a sense of enjoyment rather than out of a sense of obligation or guilt.

If you are able to use empathic responses even occasionally, you'll be giving your children a new model for communicating with their peers, siblings and teachers, as well as with you. It may become so natural to them that they won't need parenting books or courses when they are adults! Six-year-old Susan already seems headed in that direction:

Susan's father had been practicing the skills he had learned in the workshop for some time. One evening when his wife was out and he was exhausted, he struggled mightily with three-year-old Guy about getting ready for bed. After a half hour of what he called Guy's "dramatic whine and kvetch, interspersed with some heavy bellyaching," Dad tried to get pajamas on Guy while his sister, Susan, watched intently from the upper bunk bed. When Dad had had his fill of Guy's kicking and squirming, he gave him a spanking. Guy whined louder. Dad took aim for another whack—knowing immediately that he was functioning on automatic, but unable to stop himself.

Susan: Daddy, hitting is not permitted. If Guy doesn't listen to you, you can give him a consequence. Explain to him what will happen if he doesn't listen. You can put him in the hallway (*the family's usual place for outcasting troublemakers*). But hitting isn't permitted.

Dad: (*dumbfounded for a moment*) Yes, Susan, you are absolutely right. Thank you for reminding me.

Dad: (*turning to Guy*) I'm sorry I lost my temper. I was angry because I couldn't make you be still long enough to get you ready for bed. I shouldn't have hit you. Hitting isn't permitted. I love you, Guy.

Guy: I love you too, Daddy.

And there were hugs and kisses all around.

SELECTIONS FOR FURTHER READING

Briggs, Dorothy C. *Your Child's Self-Esteem*. New York: Doubleday, 1970.
Based on the belief that a healthy self-concept is the source of psychological well-being, Briggs's focus is on helping parents develop this quality in their children.

Dodson, Fitzhugh. *How to Discipline with Love*. New York: New American Library, 1978.
Many practical strategies that suggest specific ways to deal with children's behavior from birth through adolescence.

Dreikurs, Rudolf, and Soltz, Vicki. *Children, the Challenge*. New York: Dutton, 1964.
Dreikurs, a student of Alfred Adler, presents techniques to help parents diminish conflict. Of particular interest are his chapters on siblings, the use of consequences and the disadvantages of reward and punishment.

Faber, Adele, and Mazlish, Elaine. *Liberated Parents—Liberated Children*. New York: Grosset & Dunlap, 1974.
Two mothers who studied with Haim Ginott relate their successes and failures with warmth and conviction. A moving book with which parents can identify.

———. *How to Talk So Kids Will Listen and Listen So Kids Will Talk*. New York: Rawson-Wade, 1980.
A follow-up to *Liberated Parents—Liberated Children*, this concentrates more on specific techniques of communication with children.

Fraiberg, Selma. *The Magic Years.* New York: Scribners, 1959.
In clear jargon-free prose, Fraiberg helps parents grasp the basic psychoanalytic concepts as they apply to the first six years. An important book in understanding children's emotional development.

Ginott, Haim. *Between Parent and Child.* New York: Macmillan, 1965.
The inspiration for many of the ideas in my book began with Ginott who was one of the first psychologists to emphasize the need for caring, skillful communication with children.

————. *Between Parent and Teenager.* New York: Macmillan, 1969.
This is still the book I prefer for parents of teenagers because it combines an understanding of adolescent behavior with specific, practical advice.

————. *Teacher and Child.* New York: Macmillan, 1972.
Helpful for parents as well as teachers, particularly as it relates to school problems, homework and enhancing teacher-child relationships.

Gordon, Thomas. *P.E.T., Parent Effectiveness Training.* New York: Peter Wyden, 1970.
A very structured approach to communication skills, with similarities to Ginott, and some differences (such as Gordon's discussion of parental anger and setting limits).

Kersey, Katherine. *Sensitive Parenting.* Washington, D.C.: Acropolis Press, 1983.
A positive and down-to-earth approach that supplements many of the ideas in this book. Contains interesting examples.

Lerman, Saf. *Parent Awareness: Positive Parenting for the 1980's.* Minneapolis: Winston Press, 1981.
A humane view of children that seeks to help parents discipline with compassion.

LeShan, Eda. *When Your Child Drives You Crazy.* New York:

St. Martin's Press, 1985.

A variety of essays about the pains and pleasures of being a parent presented in LeShan's warm, personal style. Valuable insights into everyday problems.

Other Books You May Find Helpful

Ames, Louise B. *He Hit Me First: When Brothers and Sisters Fight*. New York: Dembner Books, 1983.

Offers many hints on how to diminish parent involvement in sibling squabbles, and includes useful information about child development.

Ames, Louise B., and Chase, Joan Ames. *Don't Push Your Preschooler*. Rev. ed. New York: Harper & Row, 1980.

The title tells you what Ames has discovered after many years of research at the Gesell Institute of Child Development. The book tells you why not to push and what to do instead.

Atkin, Edith, and Rubin, Estelle. *Part-Time Father*. New York: Vanguard Press, 1976.

As a support to fathers who are in the process of divorce or separation, this clear and useful book fills an important gap. Helpful to mothers as well.

Axline, Virginia. *Play Therapy*. Boston: Houghton Mifflin, 1947.

A pioneer in the use of play therapy for children, Axline offers insights into the art of acknowledging feelings.

Balter, Lawrence. *Dr. Balter's Child Sense: Understanding and Handling the Common Problems of Infancy and Early Childhood*. New York: Poseidon Press, 1985.

Dr. Balter talks to parents of young children in ways that are supportive and nonjudgmental and gives practical advice about many common problems.

Bank, Stephen, and Kahn, Michael. *The Sibling Bond*. New York: Basic Books, 1983.

This book is a thoughtful examination of the many combinations and complexities of the sibling bond from birth through old age.

Bergstrom, Joan. *School's Out: Now What?* Berkeley, Calif.: Ten Speed Press, 1984.

An immensely practical book that gives parents concrete suggestions and extensive resources for helping children make the most of their free time.

*Bernstein, Anne. *The Flight of the Stork.* New York: Dell, 1978.

A sound, straightforward book for parents who want to understand and respond helpfully to children's questions about sexuality at different ages and stages.

Brazelton, T. Berry. *Toddlers and Parents.* New York: Delacorte, 1969.

One of America's most respected, authoritative pediatricians reassures parents about the normal, expectable parameters of toddlerhood.

————. *To Listen to a Child: Understanding the Normal Problems of Growing Up.* Reading, Pa.: Addison-Wesley, 1984.

An informed approach to some of the emotional and physical problems encountered in the process of children's growth.

*Brenton, Myron. *How to Survive Your Child's Rebellious Teens.* New York: Lippincott, 1979.

Helps parents distinguish between normal adolescent behavior and serious acting-out. A sensible well-balanced approach.

Burck, Frances Wells. *Mothers Talking: Sharing the Secret.* New York: St. Martin's Press, 1986.

A moving portrayal of the intensity and diversity of the mothering experience as told by mothers in their own words.

---

*The books marked with an asterisk are currently out of print, but check your local library.

Calladine, Andrew and Carole. *Raising Brothers and Sisters Without Raising the Roof.* Minneapolis: Winston Press, 1983. One of the most straightforward books to help parents deal with sibling dilemmas on a day-to-day basis. Contains many specific suggestions.

Chess, Stella, Thomas, Alexander; and Birch, Herbert. *Your Child Is a Person: A Psychological Approach to Parenthood without Guilt.* New York: Viking, 1965; New York: Penguin, 1977. This nonblaming approach, based on long-term studies, stresses the importance of temperament as a guide to understanding children.

Davitz, Lois and Joel. *How to Live (Almost) Happily with a Teenager.* Minneapolis: Winston Press, 1982. This approach helps parents deal with their adolescents in a rational, well-thought-out manner.

Franke, Linda B. *Growing Up Divorced.* New York: Linden Press, 1983. One of the best of many books on this subject. Contains important insights lucidly expressed.

Galinsky, Ellen. *Between Generations: The Six Stages of Parenthood.* New York: Times Books, 1981. An innovative description of the ways in which parents change and grow as they pass through the different stages of their children's development.

Gardner, Richard A. *The Boys and Girls Book about Divorce.* New York: Bantam Books, 1971. Although written for children, this book is useful for parents as well. Contains many insights into the strong, ambivalent feelings accompanying divorce and separation.

————. *The Boys and Girls Book about One-Parent Families.* New York: Bantam Books, 1983. One of the most helpful books for parents and children on the topic of the single-parent family.

*Harrison-Ross, Phyllis, and Peter Wyden, Barbara. *The Black

Child: A Parent's Guide. New York: Peter Wyden, 1973.
Valuable insights into the conscious and unconscious attitudes toward race that affect children, both black and white.

Hechinger, Grace. *How to Raise a Street-Smart Child.* New York: Facts on File, 1984.
One of the most sensible and rational of the many books to appear on all aspects of child safety.

*Heffner, Elaine. *Mothering: The Emotional Experience after Freud and Feminism.* New York: Doubleday, 1978.
An eloquent and thoughtful discussion of the ambivalent feelings accompanying motherhood. The chapters on anger and guilt are particularly helpful.

Hirschmann, Jane, and Zaphiropoulos, Lela. *Are You Hungry? A Completely New Approach to Raising Children Free of Food and Weight Problems.* New York: Random House, 1985.
A novel approach that challenges many of the eating myths that parents of previous generations imposed upon their children. Thoughtful and provocative.

Jablow, Martha M. *Cara: Growing with a Retarded Child.* Philadelphia: Temple University Press, 1982.
Both a moving personal account of raising a child with Down's syndrome and a vitally important guide for any parent bringing up a retarded child.

Kaplan, Louise. *Oneness and Separateness: From Infant to Individual.* New York: Simon & Schuster, 1978.
A poetic and clear explanation of Margaret Mahler's approach to the psychological development of the first three years.

Klagsbrun, Francine. *Married People: Staying Together in the Age of Divorce.* New York: Bantam Books, 1985. A wise and important contribution to our understanding of the many elements that make marriages work over time.

Lansky, Vicki. *Practical Parenting Tips.* Deephaven, Minn.: Meadowbrook Press, 1980.

A "nuts and bolts" collection of practical hints and ideas discovered by parents in their on-the-job training.

————. *Practical Parenting Tips for the School-Age Years*. New York: Bantam Books, 1985.

Same as her *Practical Parenting Tips* but directed toward parents of children 6–10.

Lappé, Frances Moore. *What to Do after You Turn Off the TV*. New York: Ballantine Books, 1985.

Like many other parents, the author worried about the negative effects of television on her children. In this engaging book, she gives parents concrete alternatives that suggest what to do in place of TV.

Lofas, Jeannette, and Roosevelt, Ruth. *Living in Step*. New York: McGraw-Hill, 1977.

A down-to-earth, realistic discussion of the potential pitfalls of being a stepparent. One of the better books on this subject.

McBride, Angela B. *The Growth and Development of Mothers*. New York: Barnes & Noble, 1973.

An insightful discussion of guilt, ambivalence and the many myths that accompany the mothering experience.

McCoy, Kathy, and Wibbelsman, Charles. *The Teenage Body Book*. Rev. ed. New York: Pocket Books, Wallaby, 1984.

Immensely helpful for both teens and their parents. Comprehensive in scope and written with clarity and candor.

Miller, Alice. *For Your Own Good: Hidden Cruelty in Childrearing and the Roots of Violence*. New York: Farrar, Straus & Giroux, 1983.

A dramatic and powerful indictment of what Miller, a Swiss analyst, calls "poisonous pedagogy," in which harsh parental discipline is passed on from one generation to the next.

Napier, Augustus, and Whitaker, Carl. *The Family Crucible*. New York: Harper & Row, 1978.

One of the most interesting and readable books about the process of family therapy.

Norris, Gloria, and Miller, JoAnn. *The Working Mother's Complete Handbook*. Rev. ed. New York: New American Library, 1984.
A useful and comprehensive guide for parents working outside of the home.

Pomeranz, Virginia E., with Dodi Shultz. *The First Five Years*. New York: St. Martin's Press, 1984.
No-nonsense advice from a practicing pediatrician.

Reit, Seymour. *Sibling Rivalry*. New York: Ballantine Books, 1985.
Factual, realistic and reassuring information for dealing with the inevitability of sibling rivalry.

Satir, Virginia. *Peoplemaking*. Palo Alto, Calif.: Science & Behavior Books, 1972.
An innovative and original look at family dynamics.

Schiff, Harriet S. *The Bereaved Parent*. New York: Penguin, 1977.
A moving book by a parent who experienced the death of a child. Helpful not only to parents who have undergone this tragedy, but to their friends and relatives as well.

Spock, Benjamin, and Rothenberg, Michael. *Dr. Spock's Baby and Child Care*. Rev. ed. New York: Pocket Books, 1985.
Still the most complete reference book for accurate information about the physical and emotional health of children.

Trelease, Jim. *The Read-Aloud Handbook*. New York: Penguin, 1982.
This book is a must for any parent who wants to help his child learn to love reading. Helpful, specific, innovative ideas to make reading irresistible from birth through pre-adolescence.

Turecki, Stanley, and Tonner, Leslie. *The Difficult Child*. New York: Bantam Books, 1985.

Dr. Turecki spells out a specific program for dealing with the temperamentally difficult child. Refreshingly free of blame toward either parent or child.

Viorst, Judith. *Necessary Losses*. New York: Simon and Schuster, 1986.

Wise and thought-provoking essays about growth and change in relationships, in which Viorst synthesizes psychoanalytic theory, vivid interviews and personal experience. Compelling and informative.

Visher, John and Emily. *Stepfamilies: A Guide to Working with Stepparents and Stepchildren*. New York: Bruner, Mazel, 1979.

Written by therapists who are themselves stepparents (of eight children), this is an authoritative guide for both parents and professionals.

————. *How to Win as a Stepfamily*. Chicago: Contemporary Books, 1982.

Down-to-earth advice for stepparents, plus an excellent bibliography for children as well as parents.

Wallerstein, Judith S., and Kelly, Joan B. *Surviving the Breakup: How Children and Parents Cope with Divorce*. New York: Basic Books, 1980.

Based on one of the most complete, long-term studies of the effects of divorce on children of different ages, this book is valuable for parents and therapists as well.

*Weisberger, Eleanor. *Your Young Child and You: How to Manage Growing-up Problems in the Years from One to Five*. New York: Dutton, 1975.

Practical, readable and simple without being simplistic.

Weiss, Joan S. *Your Second Child: A Guide for Parents*. New York: Summit Books, 1981.

A detailed look at the impact of the second child on the family. Provides a good balance between theory and practice, and discusses the advantages and disadvantages of having more than one child.

AUTHOR'S NOTE

I am eager to hear from you and welcome your comments, reactions and suggestions. Let me know what worked for you and what difficulties you may have encountered. Or if you wish to learn more about Parent Guidance Workshops, please write to me, Nancy Samalin, c/o Viking Penguin, 40 West 23 Street, New York, N.Y. 10010. Thank you.

INDEX